NUTSHELLS

CONSTITUTIONAL AND ADMINISTRATIVE LAW IN A NUTSHELL

NUTSHELLS

CONSTITUTIONAL AND ADMINISTRATIVE LAW IN A NUTSHELL

SEVENTH EDITION

by

GREER HOGAN, LL.B., M.A.
Associate Dean, Law School,
University of Northumbria

London • Sweet & Maxwell • 2005

First Edition 1987
Second Edition 1990
Third Edition 1993
Fourth Edition 1996
Fifth Edition 1998
Sixth Edition 2002
Reprinted 2002
Reprinted 2003

Published in 2005 by Sweet & Maxwell Limited of
100 Avenue Road, London NW3 3PF
Typeset by LBJ Typesetting Ltd of Kingsclere
Printed in Wales by Creative Print and Design Group

No natural forests were destroyed to make this product.
Only farmed timber was used and replanted.

A CIP catalogue record for this book is available
from the British Library.

ISBN 0 421 890 908

CONTENTS

1. THE NATURE OF THE CONSTITUTION

Most countries have a written document known as "the constitution" which lays down the main rules governing the structure and functions of government, which regulates the relationship between the state and its citizens and provides a measure of the legitimacy of government actions. Typically such constitutions are to some degree entrenched, that is, the constitutional rules are more difficult to change than ordinary laws, perhaps requiring approval by referendum (Republic of Ireland) or special majority (United States of America). Such constitutions also tend to have a higher status than ordinary laws thus creating the need for a supreme body such as a supreme court with the power to declare laws passed in contravention of the constitution, invalid.

CHARACTERISTICS OF THE BRITISH CONSTITUTION

Unwritten

In Britain we do not have a written constitution in the sense of a formal document but that does not mean that we lack constitutional rules. These are expressed with differing degrees of formality in the form of statutory provisions, case law and conventions of the constitution.

There are, compared to many countries, few positive statements regarding the powers and duties of the organs of government. These are simply recognised by common law and convention and are subject to various legal and conventional limitations. Our constitution historically did not contain any positive declaration of the rights of individuals in the form of a Bill of Rights. Those rules relating to such matters as freedom of speech and assembly were traditionally derived from, and had the same status as, any other rule of law. The Human Rights Act 1998 (HRA) has had the effect of incorporating the European Convention on Human Rights (ECHR) into our law and giving individuals rights which can be directly enforced in the UK courts.

Flexible

The British Constitution can be described as flexible in that:

(a) It does not have the rigidity of most written constitutions as Parliament can repeal any law by a simple majority. The orthodox viewpoint is that, as each successive Parliament has the power to pass or repeal any legislation, any attempt to bind Parliament by entrenching a statutory provision, would be ineffective (*Ellen Street Estates Ltd v Minister of Health* (CA, 1936)). It has, however, been argued that certain fundamental Acts of Parliament such as the Act of Union with Scotland 1707 and the European Communities Act 1972 could not be repealed as, in each case, Parliament which enacted the provision is no longer in existence in the same form but has reconstituted itself as a less powerful body. In *Thoburn v Sunderland City Council* (DC, 2001), Laws L.J. expressed the view that within our law there was a hierarchy of Acts of Parliament, ordinary statutes and constitutional statutes, and that while the former may be impliedly repealed, the latter, such as the European Communities Act, could only be repealed expressly.

In any event, while in legal theory there may be complete flexibility, the political reality may be quite different. The Statute of Westminster 1931, the various Independence Acts may, in theory, be capable of repeal, but in practice they are entrenched in our constitution. "Freedom once given cannot be taken away. Legal theory must give way to practical politics" (*per* Lord Denning in *Blackburn v The Att-Gen* (CA, 1971)).

Some writers have also argued that there are inherent limitations on what Parliament can or cannot do and that it does not have the power to pass laws contrary to fundamental human values. If, for example, it legislated to provide that "all blue eyed babies should be killed" then Lord Woolf has argued that the courts would simply refuse to uphold the law.

(b) The absence of a written constitution has allowed quite considerable changes to be made informally, without amendment of these legal rules which do exist. For example, the gradual transfer of power from the House of Commons to the Cabinet occurred without any formal legislative change. Conventions, an important source of constitutional law can be extremely flexible, reflecting changes in the political situation as and when they occur. Thus the constitution can evolve gradually.

Unitary

Because all legislative power stems from Parliament, we have a unitary as opposed to a federal constitution. It is certainly possible for Parliament to give limited powers of government to local authorities and to local and national assemblies but the doctrine of parliamentary sovereignty means that a subsequent Parliament can repeal the relevant legislation and take back the power. For example this happened in 1972 when the Westminster Parliament reimposed direct rule in Northern Ireland and in 2000 when the Northern Ireland Assembly established under the Northern Ireland Act 1998 was suspended after the IRA failed to decommission its weapons.

A Scottish Parliament was established by the Scotland Act 1998. The major areas reserved for the UK Parliament are the constitution, the registration of political parties, foreign affairs, civil service, defence and treason. Nor can the Scottish Parliament amend such acts as the Scotland Act, the European Communities Act 1972 and the HRA (Schs 4 and 5). Under Pt IV of the Act the Scottish Parliament has the power to vary the basic rate of tax byup to three pence in the pound.

The Welsh Assembly, established by the Government of Wales Act 1998 has much more limited powers. These are of an executive rather than a legislative nature.

SOURCES OF THE CONSTITUTION

Legislation

Although we do not have a written constitution there are many Acts of Parliament relevant to constitutional law. Some fundamental steps in the constitutional development of the country were the Bill of Rights 1689 which limited the power of the monarch to rule by virtue of the royal prerogative, the Act of Settlement 1700 which further strengthened the power of Parliament and provided for the succession to the English throne, the European Communities Act 1972 which took this country into what is now known as the European Union (EU) and the HRA. The composition of Parliament has been altered by the House of Lords Act 1999 and its powers by the Parliament Acts 1911 and 1949.

Case law

According to Dicey, writing in the nineteenth century, the British Constitution was "judge made". Even today there are many areas of constitutional law regulated not by statute but by the common law as expounded by our judges. Examples of this can be seen in the development of the doctrine of the supremacy of Parliament and, in judicial review, the establishment of a right to a fair hearing.

In recent years there has been an increased reliance on statute law, for example, in relation to public order and the powers of the police, but, of course, here too, the judges have a role to play in the interpretation of the statutory provisions.

Conventions of the Constitution

If one tries to understand the British Constitution simply by reference to case law and statute, one obtains a totally false impression. Take one example, the role played by the monarch. The Queen must give the royal assent to all legislation. She appoints the Prime Minister and has the power to dissolve Parliament. This might lead one to believe that the monarch still exercises considerable political power. Yet in practice we now have a constitutional monarchy where the Queen acts on the advice of her Prime Minister. The royal assent has not been refused since 1708. No monarch has refused to dissolve Parliament in modern times and the Queen has, in recent years, been relieved of any real responsibility as to the choice of Prime Minister as the various political parties have now clearly defined rules for the election of a leader.

Such changes in the power of the monarch have arisen, not through statute, but as a result of the convention that the monarch should not become politically involved and should not be seen to favour any one political party.

This example illustrates the fact that the formal rules have to be understood against a background of constitutional conventions which can both expand and modify the strict legal rules. And so conventions have been described as "the flesh which clothes the dry bones of the law".

What are conventions?

(a) Conventions are non-legal rules of constitutional behaviour which are considered to be binding upon those who operate the constitution but which are not enforced by the courts or by the presiding officers in Parliament. They may be recognised by the courts as part of the constitutional background against which a particular decision is taken (*Carltona v Commissioners of Works* (CA, 1943)), but will not be enforced directly. (See also *Reference Re Amendment of the Constitution of Canada* (Supreme Court of Canada 1982)).

(b) They are not written down in any formal sense in that they are not expressed as Acts of Parliament nor are they established by judicial precedent. Occasionally an existing convention is formalised as, for example, s.43 of the Statute of Westminster 1931.

(c) Important constitutional institutions such as the Cabinet and the office of Prime Minister have been created by convention. The first statutory reference to the Prime Minister came in the Chequers Estate Act 1917. The relationship between Government and Parliament can only be understood against the background of the convention of ministerial responsibility. They thus have a central role in the development of the British Constitution.

Advantages and disadvantages of conventions

While the use of conventions can add flexibility to our constitutional rules and avoid the constant need for formal change to ensure the constitution properly reflects the realities of political life, it does provide the government with easy opportunities to amend the rules in its favour.

Other sources

The law of the European Union

By virtue of our membership of the European Union, community law is part of our law. The primary sources of community law are the Treaties, for example the three founding Treaties and the Treaty of European Union. The secondary sources are regulations, directives, decisions of the Council and the Commission and the jurisprudence of the European Court of Justice.

ECHR law

An increasingly important source of public law is the European Convention for the Protection of Human Rights and Fundamental Freedoms.

There have been numerous cases in recent years where individuals have had to apply to the European Court of Human Rights to assert their fundamental rights. (See for example, *Findlay v UK* (1997) on the fairness of courts martial proceedings and *Halford v UK* (1997) on violation of rights of privacy).

Not only was it politically embarrassing to have to go outside this country to enforce rights guaranteed under the ECHR, "exhibiting our dirty linen in public", it was also an expensive, time consuming process.

The Human Rights Act 1998 does not attempt to incorporate the ECHR into English law, in the sense of giving it a higher status than other laws. It achieves effective incorporation largely through the rule of statutory interpretation in s.3(1) which provides that, in so far as it is possible to do so, legislation must be given effect to in a way which is compatible with the Convention rights. In doing this, the court must take into account relevant decisions and opinions of the European Court of Human Rights. This means that UK judges must now attempt to interpret legislation in a convention compliant manner even where this may be at odds with the likely intention of Parliament. This applies irrespective of when the legislation was passed. *Antonio Mendoza v Ahmad Raja Ghaidan* (HL, 2004) provides an example of the court departing from an earlier interpretation of a statutory provision relating to the tenancy rights of the survivor of a homosexual couple. It was now necessary to take into account Convention rights and it was possible to re-interpret the section to make it convention compliant.

The courts cannot declare any law invalid as being in conflict with the convention. Rather, under s.4 the superior courts can make a declaration of incompatibility where a provision of primary or subordinate legislation is not convention compliant. This does not, of itself, affect the validity of the legislation nor is it binding on the parties to the instant case. A number of such declarations have now been made, for example in *Wilson v First County Securities* (CA, 2001) it was found that s.127(3) of the Consumer Credit Act 1974 was incompatible with Art.6 of the ECHR.

Following a finding of incompatibility government ministers can use a fast track procedure in s.10 to amend the law by using subordinate legislation. This happened, for example, after incompatibility had been found between s.73 of the Mental Health Act 1983 and Art.5 of the ECHR. While not without precedent, the power to amend primary legislation by ministerial order is highly unusual and some critics have said that it sets a very dangerous precedent which could lead to a considerable increase in executive power.

Section 6 of the Act provides that it is unlawful for any public body to act in a way which is incompatible with a Convention right. While the term "public body" includes courts, government bodies, local authorities and the police, it does not include Parliament itself. The inclusion of courts in the definition means that the Act has both horizontal and vertical effect. The Act can be used both as a shield and as a sword.

Any victim of such an unlawful act can bring judicial review proceedings in our courts or rely on the Convention right in any legal proceedings he is involved in, for example, by using the right as a defence in criminal proceedings. Only where the public body is required by legislation to act as it did would its action be safe from challenge.

No special courts or remedies have been created. Nor does the Act introduce any criminal penalties for non compliance with the provisions.

Parliamentary supremacy is maintained as the Act does not prevent Parliament passing legislation conflicting with the Convention. It does, however, require a Minister in charge of a Bill to make a statement before the Second Reading either to the effect that, in his view, the provisions of the Bill are compatible with the Convention rights, (a statement of compatibility), or conversely that, although he cannot make such a statement, the Government wishes the House to proceed with the Bill.

The Act represents a compromise. The judiciary have been given the power to scrutinise legislation in the light of these rights guaranteed by the Convention but ultimate political control over the extent of these rights remains with the Government.

The law and custom of Parliament

Parliament has the right to regulate its own procedure and does so by means of standing orders. These, together with resolutions passed by either House and the rulings given by the Speaker, are contained in Erskine May's *Parliamentary Practice*.

Treaties, Conventions and other international obligations

These are not a direct source of constitutional law in the sense that they do not normally involve any change in domestic law

(See, however, *The Parlement Belge* (HC, 1879)). A treaty may bind the government in international law but will normally be given effect within this country by the passing of legislation. This happened in the case of membership of the EU where the signing of the various treaties was followed by the passing of the European Communities Act 1972. Similarly international conventions such as the ECHR, although ratified by Great Britain in 1953, did not, until the passage of the HRA in 1998, give directly enforceable rights to individuals in this country. (See *R. v Home Secretary, Ex p. Brind* (HL, 1991)). The courts will, however, have some regard for conventions presuming that Parliament intends to comply with its international obligations.

THE RULE OF LAW

The absence of a formal written constitution in the UK has meant that there is no positive statement of the basic values governing state actions, no formal guidelines which could be used as a measure of the legitimacy of government action. The concept of the rule of law has been used by lawyers and politicians in an attempt to provide such a measure. It is important to note that the rule of law is not a set of legal rules. The rule of law is not directly enforceable by the courts and there is no legal sanction for behaviour which contravenes it. It is best thought of as a guiding principle. Its precise meaning is not however entirely clear.

Dicey's concept of the Rule of Law

For Dicey there were three essential features:

"(a) It means the absolute supremacy or predominance of regular law as opposed to the influence of arbitrary power and excludes the existence of arbitrariness, of prerogative or even wide discretionary authority on the part of Government . . . a man may be punished for breach of the law but he cannot be punished for anything else.

(b) It means equality before the law, or the equal subjection of all classes to the ordinary law of the land and administered by the ordinary courts.

(c) It means the constitution is the result of the ordinary law of the land . . . the rights of the individual are secured by and enmeshed in the common law and not by a constitutional document which can be suspended by a stroke of the pen."

To what extent is the Rule of Law reflected in English Law?

Our courts have always accepted the need for officials to point to the source of their powers (*Entick v Carrington* 1765). Actions cannot be justified simply because they are official. In many respects, however, the law does not match up to Dicey's strictures. A range of arbitrary powers is available to the government under Emergency Powers and anti-terrorism legislation. Many government actions are still carried out by virtue of the royal prerogative, the limitations of which are difficult to define. (Although the courts are now prepared to control its exercise (*Council for Civil Service Unions v Minister for the Civil Service* (HL, 1984) See Ch.2). It is difficult to see how any modern government could operate without resort to the use of wide discretionary powers. The Rule of Law does alert us to the need to ensure that discretionary power is properly controlled. The courts have recognised that discretionary power is never "unfettered". (See, *e.g. Padfield v Minister of Agriculture* (HL, 1968)).

No one can be detained without proper legal authority but sometimes that authority is present in circumstances where no breach of the law has been established. An obvious example is the refusal of bail. The Anti-Terrorism, Crime and Security Act 2001 which allows the detention of suspected international terrorists by order of the Home Secretary is also a clear breach of the principle.

Dicey emphasised that no one should be above the law and the law should apply to officials and citizens alike. The privileges and immunities given to the Crown have tended to decrease over the years. The Crown Proceedings Act 1947 made it considerably easier to sue the Crown. Certain privileges and immunities remain, the personal immunity of the sovereign from being sued, the privilege of free speech granted to MPs, diplomatic immunity, for example. Note that Dicey's real concern was to distinguish us from the French system of administrative courts which he wrongly felt tended to protect the administration. The trend in recent years has been for the development of a more coherent system of administrative law in England, a distinct procedure for raising public law issues by way of applications for judicial review and the establishment of the Administrative Court developing consistent principles of public law.

Dicey clearly felt that stronger protection was given to constitutional rights by the ordinary law of the land than by a single constitutional document. His argument could be summed up colloquially by stating it was better not to put all your eggs in the one basket. Many of our constitutional rights now come from the ECHR by virtue of the Human Rights Act 1998.

Limitations of the concept

The emphasis is on the regularity and certainty of the legal rules rather than on the content of the rules although Dicey does emphasise that decisions must be taken in accordance with procedural fairness. Nevertheless he is more concerned with regular enforcement and application rather than content. Other writers have attempted to expand the concept by including such matters as guarantees of economic prosperity and freedom from hunger (Delhi Declaration 1959).

Conclusion

Adherence to the rule of law may provide a check on abuse of power. It may provide a focus for critical evaluation of the way in which power is exercised. It is not itself a comprehensive code but must be supplemented by other principles which regulate the content of the legal rules themselves.

THE SUPREMACY OF PARLIAMENT

An important characteristic of our constitution has been that Parliament, not the constitution, was the supreme legal authority. While, in the majority of states, the legislature is limited by the constitution in what it can or cannot do, our Parliament has been subject to no such legal limitation. Our courts have had no power to declare laws duly passed by Parliament invalid.

According to Blackstone "What Parliament doth, no power on earth can undo." "In theory," said Dicey, "Parliament has total power. It is sovereign."

Dicey's view of Parliamentary supremacy

(a) Parliament was competent to pass laws on any subject.

(b) Its laws could regulate the activities of anyone, anywhere.
(c) Parliament could not bind its successors as to the content, manner and form of subsequent legislation.
(d) Laws passed by Parliament could not be challenged in the courts.

The legal limitations on the scope of Parliament's power

Dicey argued that there was no legal limitation on the scope of Parliament's power. Indeed Parliament has legislated on matters affecting every aspect of our lives. It has legislated to change fundamental constitutional principles. It has lengthened and shortened its own life. Nor has it felt bound by territorial or jurisdictional limits. Parliament has legislated regarding aliens, even with regard to their activities outside British territory (The Hijacking Act 1967). Sir Ivor Jennings once said "If Parliament enacts that smoking in the streets of Paris is an offence then, in the eyes of the English Courts, it is an offence." There may be practical difficulties in enforcing such a law but that would not make it invalid.

Political considerations may make it unlikely, even inconceivable that Parliament might legislate in a particular manner. Can one imagine a situation where Parliament passed legislation regulating the internal affairs of the United States of America? This led Professor HWR Wade to argue that it was nonsensical to have a legal theory which said that Parliament could pass laws on any subject without restriction. Certainly there are many internal and external political limitations on Parliament's freedom of action.

It has been argued that British membership of the EU imposes a legal not simply a political limitation on Parliament. The 1967 White Paper (Cmnd. 3301) on the Legal and Constitutional Implications of Membership of the EC, stated that Parliament's freedom of action would be limited in that it would have to refrain from passing legislation inconsistent with community law and would be under an obligation in certain instances to legislate to give effect to our community obligations. The European Communities Act 1972, s.2(1) gives present and future community law legal force in the United Kingdom and s.2(2) provides for the implementation of community law by means of secondary legislation but the Act does not specifically prohibit Parliament from enacting conflicting legislation.

If, however, such conflicting legislation was ineffective in so far as it was inconsistent with community law, Parliament's power to legislate as it liked would be accordingly limited. McEldowney, for example, argues that such a limitation has occurred as Parliament's authority to legislate has become integrated with EC legislative policy. Certainly, in practical terms the increased co-operation required in the development of a common foreign and defence policy arising out of the Treaty on European Union and the emphasis on co-operation in home affairs is an ever increasing fetter on the Westminster Parliament's freedom of action.

The power of Parliament to bind its successors

The courts have long accepted Dicey's view that Parliament has no power to bind its successors either as to the manner or as to the form of subsequent legislation. As each successive Parliament is deemed to be all powerful, logically, that Parliament must have the power to make or unmake any law. Accordingly it would seem to be impossible to entrench a provision in our constitution.

It was said in *Godden v Hales* (1686) that Parliament was entitled to ignore any provision in an earlier Act purporting to prevent the Act being repealed in the normal way, that is either expressly or by implication. This was followed in the case of *Ellen Street Estates Ltd v The Minister of Health* (CA, 1934) where the court found that it was impossible for Parliament to enact that, in a subsequent statute dealing with the same subjectmatter, there should be no implied repeal. "The one thing Parliament cannot do is to bind its successor" (Maughan L.J.).

Various arguments have been put forward to suggest that specific statutory provisions have been entrenched.

The Statute of Westminster: Independence Acts

It has been argued that these have been entrenched as, in terms of the political realities of the situation, it is inconceivable that Parliament would repeal them. (Lord Denning M.R. in *Blackburn v The Att-Gen* (CA, 1971)).

That is not to say that if, in the future, Parliament did repeal an Independence Act and passed legislation purporting to regulate the internal affairs of the country, the British courts would reject such legislation. In *Madzimbamuto v Lardner Burke* (PC, 1969) Lord Reid said that even if Parliament acted improperly or unwisely, it was not open to the courts to say that it had acted illegally and that the resultant legislation was invalid. The court advised that a detention order made under the authority of an Emergency Powers Act passed by the illegal regime in Rhodesia was invalid as that regime's authority to legislate had been taken away. It did not allow the political reality of the situation to affect its conclusion knowing full well that the detention order would continue to be upheld within Rhodesia. In practical terms it was impossible to provide a remedy for the detained Madzimbamuto. The case did, of course, involve a limited grant of independence. Rhodesia was not a sovereign state.

Where such a sovereign state has been created by a grant of independence, the courts may be more reluctant to take back power in that they would have to recognise the political fact that the state in question was a foreign country and no longer part of the legal order of this country. Yet within our legal system, Parliament appears to have the legal power to repeal any law, even to act contrary to the principles of international law. The courts would simply uphold the latest intention of Parliament. (See Lord Sankey L.C. in *British Coal Corp. v The King* (HL, 1935) and Sir Robert Megarry V.C. in *Manuel v Att-Gen* (HC, 1983)).

The European Communities Act 1972

Several grounds have been suggested for holding that this Act cannot be repealed:

(a) That by joining the European Economic Community, a new order was created. Within that new order Parliament is no longer all powerful and cannot amend or repeal any statute by which that order was established. The European Communities Act, it is argued, is such a constituent statute, and is accordingly entrenched. (A similar argument has been used with regard to the Act of Union between Scotland and England in 1707).

(b) That by assigning rights and powers to the community in accordance with the Treaty provisions Member States have limited their sovereign rights in such a way as to make it impossible to withdraw unilaterally (*Art Treasures Case* (EC, 1972)).

There is no evidence to suggest that the British courts would accept this view Lord Denning in *Macarthy Ltd v Smith* (CA, 1979) clearly envisaged that Parliament could repeal the 1972 Act although it would have to be done expressly and not by implication. The political view is clearly that a right to withdraw exists.

(c) That, ultimately, the validity of legislation depends on the rules of recognition employed by our judges. The present norm of validity recognises the latest statutory intention of Parliament. It has been suggested that this norm has altered and that the courts will recognise as valid only legislation which has been passed by both houses and given the royal assent, has not been repealed expressly or by implication and which accords with our obligations under community law. (It has been suggested that one method by which a written constitution could be entrenched could be by "manufacturing" such a change in the norm of validity by altering the terms of the judicial oath so that judges would swear to uphold only laws which were in conformity with the constitutional provisions—per HWR Wade, 1989 Hamlyn Lecture: *Constitutional Fundamentals*).

A Limitation on the Doctrine of Implied Repeal

In *Thoburn v Sunderland City Council* (QB, 2001), Laws L.J. stated that the common law had come to recognise that there were certain fundamental constitutional rights and thus a hierarchy of Acts of Parliament, ordinary statutes and constitutional statutes. While ordinary statutes may be repealed by implication, the latter can only be repealed by express words on the face of the statute. The European Communities Act was such a statute.

Laws passed by Parliament cannot be challenged in the courts

Traditionally our courts have refused to consider the validity of an Act of Parliament either on the ground that Parliament had no power to pass it or on the ground that the statute had been improperly passed.

Substantive validity

Until the seventeenth century the courts would declare Acts of Parliament void if they considered them contrary to natural law, repugnant to the law or impossible to be performed. In modern times any such challenge has been totally unsuccessful.

In *R. v Jordan* (1967), Jordan, who had been sentenced for offences under the Race Relations Act 1965, applied for a writ of habeas corpus claiming that he had been convicted under an invalid law. He alleged that the statute in question was invalid in that it conflicted with a fundamental principle of natural law, the right of free speech. He claimed that no Act of Parliament could take away this right.

The argument was rejected by the court which simply stated that it had no power to consider the validity of an Act of Parliament. This view was endorsed by the House of Lords in *British Rail Board v Pickin* (HL, 1974) and followed in *Martin v O'Sullivan* (CA, 1982).

In order to maintain parliamentary supremacy the Human Rights Act does not give the courts any power to declare legislation invalid where it conflicts with the ECHR but simply allows the court to make a declaration of incompatibility (s.4). The onus is then on Parliament to change the law if it so wishes.

Procedural irregularity

Acts of Parliament have also been challenged on the ground that they have been improperly passed. In 1842 a Private Act of Parliament was challenged on this ground *(Edinburgh & Dalkeith Railway v Wauchope* (HL, 1842)). Lord Campbell, upholding the validity of the Act, refused to investigate the internal workings of Parliament saying that if the Act appeared valid on its face, then it must be accepted by the courts. If, from the Parliamentary Roll it appeared that the Bill had passed through both Houses and received the Royal Assent, the courts could not inquire into what happened during its parliamentary stages. That is a question for Parliament.

A number of writers have sought to distinguish such a procedural challenge from the substantive challenge in cases such as *Jordan* arguing that it does not seek to limit Parliament's area of power. It can be argued that there is a clear difference between finding that Parliament has failed to follow its own procedural rules and from saying that Parliament does not have the power to legislate in a particular way. RFV Heuston summarises this by saying that there is a distinction between the rules which govern on the one hand the composition and the procedure and, on the other hand, the area of power, of a sovereign legislature.

The Judicial Committee of the Privy Council appeared to give some support to this distinction. In *Att-Gen for New South Wales*

v Trethowan (PC, 1932) a decision of the Australian Supreme
Court to grant a declaration that two Bills passed by the New
South Wales State Legislature were invalid and grant an injunction restraining the Bills from being presented to the Governor
for assent was upheld. The Privy Council found that the State
Legislature was bound by s.5 of the Colonial Laws Validity Act
1865 which required any constitutional amendment to be in the
manner and form required by the legislation in force at the time.
The two Bills in question were not in the manner and form
required as under earlier State legislation any constitutional
change had to be approved by a referendum. (See also the South
African case of *Harris v Minister of the Interior* (1952)). But the
House of Lords in Pickin's case (above) clearly rejected any sort
of challenge to validity.

MEMBERSHIP OF THE EU—ITS EFFECT ON PARLIAMEN-
TARY SUPREMACY

In the view of the European Court, the courts of the Member
States should give supremacy to Community law (*Costa v ENEL,
1964*).

The 1967 White Paper on membership at para.23, states the
Government's intention to be that "Community law takes prece-
dence over the domestic law of the member states." Such an
approach is essential to ensure the necessary harmonisation of
the laws of the Member States.

Section 2(4) of the Act provides ". . . any enactment passed or
to be passed, other than one contained in this Part of this Act,
shall be construed and have effect subject to the foregoing
provisions of this section . . .". This refers back to s.2(1) which
incorporates Community law into our system. Section 2(4) could
therefore be said to give supremacy to Community law. But it
can also be held to mean no more than it creates a presumption
that, if there is a conflict between Community and domestic law,
any ambiguity in that domestic law will be resolved to give
effect to our Community obligations.

Initially the English courts took the view that English law and
Community law were of equal status and that, by the doctrine
of implied repeal, the courts should give effect to whatever
represented the latest intention of Parliament. (See, *e.g. Bulmer
(HP) Ltd v J Bollinger SA* (CA, 1974)). Indeed on many occasions
the approach was to avoid the problem altogether by treating
s.2(4) simply as a principle of construction. So in *Garland v BR*

Engineering Co (HL, 1983), an alleged conflict between s.6(4) of the Sex Discrimination Act 1975 and Art.119 of the Treaty and subsequent directives, was resolved by construing the Act widely. (See also the approach in *Duke v GEC Reliance* (HL, 1988) and *Pickstone v Freemans Plc* (HL, 1989)).

Even where the courts indicated that priority should be given to Community law, our courts attempted to uphold the traditional view on sovereignty by arguing that Community law "is not supplanting English law. It is part of our law which overrides any other part which is inconsistent with it" *(per* Lord Denning M.R. in *Macarthys v Smith* (CA, 1981)). But where there is clear indication that Parliament did not intend to fulfil its obligations under the Treaty and intentionally and expressly acted inconsistently with it, Lord Denning felt it was the duty of our courts to follow the domestic statutes.

The courts seem finally to have accepted a modification of Dicey's approach in *R. v The Secretary of State for Transport, Ex p. Factortame Ltd* (HL, 1990). Following the introduction of fishing quotas by the EC, Britain attempted to protect the interest of its fishermen by enacting the Merchant Shipping Act 1988. This prevented foreign nationals from securing part of the British quota by quota-hopping, for example by registering a company in this country. A number of Spanish fishermen who had been utilising part of the British quota by such methods, challenged the validity of the Merchant Shipping Act on the grounds that it violated their rights under Community Law. A preliminary ruling was requested under Art.177. In the meantime they applied for interim relief. The House of Lords in *Factortame 1* (1989) refused to grant interim relief (See Ch.7). It did, however, recognise that if the European Court ruled in favour of the applicants, the English courts would have to find a remedy and this might mean refusing to apply the provisions of the Merchant Shipping Act. On a further reference (*Factortame 2* (1991)), the Court of Justice reiterated the well established principle of Community law that a national court must set aside a domestic law which prevented Community law from having full effect. The matter then came back to the House of Lords in 1990. On this occasion their lordships granted interim relief to prevent the Act being enforced on the basis that the applicants had shown a strong *prima facie* case and the other grounds for granting interim relief had been met.

Thus the House of Lords had effectively suspended the operation of the Merchant Shipping Act by accepting that, where there was a conflict, Community law must prevail. By granting interim relief against the Crown they had further ignored the Crown Proceedings Act 1947 which preserved the common law rule which precluded the granting of such relief. In the subsequent Scottish case of *Murray v Rogers* (1992) the Court of Session refused to challenge the validity of the Scottish community charge legislation, saying they had normally no power to consider whether an Act of Parliament was valid unless it was incompatible with Community law.

In *R. v Secretary of State for Employment Ex p. EOC* (HL, 1994), Lord Keith said that the effect of the *Factortame* decisions was that certain provisions of UK primary legislation could be held to be invalid in their purported application to nationals of Member States of the EU.

Factortame 1 did, however, leave open the question raised by Lord Denning M.R. in *Macarthys* as to whether the British Parliament retained the power to legislate expressly in contravention of British treaty obligations. The effectiveness of any such legislation will, however, be limited.

(In 1991 the ECJ ruled on the substantive application that the Merchant Shipping Act was incompatible with the Treaty).

---

2. THE EXECUTIVE

The executive is responsible for the initiation, formulation, direction and implementation of general government policy. As will be described below decisions are taken by the Cabinet and implemented by the various government departments each headed by a government minister. Historically these powers derived from the Crown but today the monarch plays no real part in the process of government. The expression "the Crown" has become a collective term which covers not only the monarch but the actions of the executive exercising the traditional powers of the monarch to govern the country.

Nowadays the source of much power is the legislative authority of Parliament expressed through Acts of Parliament and ministers are constitutionally answerable to Parliament for the conduct of their departments. There remain, however, residual powers once exercised by the monarch personally but now exercised in the name of the Crown by government ministers. These are known as prerogative powers and are described below.

THE MONARCH

Our monarch is described as a constitutional monarch. She is Head of State, Head of the Commonwealth, Head of the Armed Forces and provides a focus for national unity. She performs a number of formal constitutional functions, giving the royal assent to legislation, opening the new Parliament, appointing the Prime Minister and a host of senior government, judicial and other public appointments. In practice, however, she has no real power as she is required to act on the advice of her Prime Minister. The last monarch, for example, to refuse to grant the Royal Assent to legislation was Queen Anne. Only a few honours remain in the personal grant of the sovereign.

Those areas where she appears to have some residual power, such as the appointment of the Prime Minister are illusory as she is entirely restricted by the convention that she approaches the leader of the party with the largest number of seats in Parliament and the parties themselves have now clearly defined methods of selecting a leader. Some political influence may remain in the power to grant or refuse a dissolution of Parliament. It is argued that in the most exceptional circumstances the monarch could thereby influence events.

Walter Bagehot writing in the nineteenth century, said that the monarch had the right to be consulted, the right to encourage and the right to warn. Prime Ministers have a weekly audience with the Queen. She receives foreign Heads of State and Ambassadors. She is supplied with copies of all cabinet papers and minutes, important Foreign Office telegrams and a summary of daily events in Parliament. Many Prime Ministers have indicated that they value the Queen's vast experience. The extent to which there is influence must remain a matter for future historians.

THE POWERS AND FUNCTIONS OF THE STATE

The state has three types of function: legislative, judicial and executive. The legislative function is exercised mainly through Parliament which has the power to make laws of general applicability and to grant to other bodies the power to make delegated legislation under authority of an act of parliament. Originally the monarch had the power to make laws by means of royal proclamation. A residue of this is the power to make *orders in council.*

The state also has the authority to determine disputes which arise out of the operation of its laws. Such disputes are allocated to courts, tribunals or even to government ministers, who, increasingly, exercise functions of a judicial nature. No clear principles determine the allocation of disputes to these bodies although the greater the element of discretion and the more important the policy considerations, the less likely it is for the courts to take on the new area of responsibility.

The state has various executive functions. It must initiate, formulate and direct general policy. That policy must then be put into operation, monitored and regulated. Responsibility for this is with the government of the country, the main decisions being taken by the Cabinet and put into effect by the various government departments and a range of quasi-autonomous bodies.

The doctrine of separation of powers

Writers, as long ago as Aristotle, have been concerned that if legislative, executive and judicial functions were concentrated in the same person or body, that body would become too powerful and would abuse its power. To avoid this they have argued that power should be distributed. One way of achieving this is by the doctrine of separation of powers where, for example, all legislative powers are concentrated in one body, all judicial powers in another and so on. Each body would then be strong enough to check and balance the power of the others. The most famous exponent of this doctrine was the French writer, Montesquieu, writing in the eighteenth century. In fact his observations on the English system of government over-emphasised the degree of separation. His views were very influential on those drafting the constitution of the United States.

There has never been a strict separation of powers in this country. Unlike the United States, the Prime Minister and the Cabinet are drawn from Parliament. Although Parliament is the main legislative organ, the courts and the executive both have legislative responsibilities. Government ministers have legislative, executive and judicial functions.

Indeed it is extremely difficult to establish any truly satisfactory system of defining the limits of these functions. Rather they seem to merge. Yet it has proved necessary to attempt this task to determine the appropriate checks and balances in the system. The courts' attitude to intervention to control any abuse of power is affected by the nature of the power being exercised. (See *Re Racal Communications Ltd* (HL, 1981) and *Vine v National Dock Labour Board* (HL, 1957)).

The doctrine is, however, of particular value in that it helps to maintain the independence of the judiciary. The effect of the Human Rights Act 1998 has also been to emphasise the need for an independent judiciary and there have been a series of cases challenging the independence of those exercising judicial functions. In *McGonnell v UK* (2000) it was found that the dual role of the Bailiff of Guernsey in approving the development plan for the area and hearing an appeal in relation to the planning process, cast doubt on his impartiality as a judge. (See also *Starrs & Chalmers v Procurator Fiscal, Linlithgow* (HCJ, 2000).

This focused concern on the role of the Lord Chancellor as presiding Officer in the House of Lords, a government minister and member of the Cabinet and a judge. The Government accordingly announced in 2003 that it intended to abolish the current role of the Lord Chancellor by such measures as the establishment of a separate Judicial Appointments Commission and the establishment of a Department of Constitutional Affairs. It has also spurred the proposal to remove the Law lords from the House of Lords and establish a separate Supreme Court. At the time of writing the Constitutional Reform Bill is in committee in the House of Lords.

Prerogative power

The powers of the state must be exercised in accordance with the law by virtue of authority granted by the law. In modern times this authority is generally granted by statute but certain powers, rights and immunities appertaining to the Crown still have their origins in the common law. These, originally exercised by the monarch personally, are known as prerogative powers.

The prerogative is a residual power and will be superseded by statute. (See *R. v Home Secretary, Ex p. Fire Brigades Union* (HL, 1995). Where the statutory provision deals with the same area, the prerogative may be extinguished either expressly or by implication. (See *Att-Gen v De Keyser's Royal Hotel* (HL, 1920). But *cf. R. v Home Secretary, Ex p. Northumbria Police Authority* (CA, 1988)).

Prerogatives may relate to the legislative, executive or judicial functions of Government. Examples of prerogatives still in existence include: the administration of overseas territories by means of orders in council; authority to make treaties; the recognition of foreign states; declarations of war and peace; the disposition and control of the armed forces; power to take action in an emergency; the prerogative of mercy; the power to stop criminal prosecutions; the granting of the royal assent to legislation; the summoning and dissolution of Parliament and the grant of Honours.

The term prerogative also includes the immunities of the crown such as the monarch's immunity from prosecution.

In the past the courts were reluctant to interfere with prerogative powers. In *Laker Airways v Department of Trade* (HC, 1976) the court indicated that while it would determine the existence and the scope of the prerogative power, it would not review the propriety or adequacy of the grounds on which it had been exercised.

However in *Council for Civil Service Unions v Minister for the Civil Service* (HL, 1984), the House of Lords recognised the possibility of reviewing the exercise of prerogative power on the same grounds as power granted under statutory provisions. It rationalised this by saying that nowadays the question of whether a power was authorised by statute or prerogative was largely a matter of historical accident. This was further recognised in cases such as *R. v Secretary of State for the Home Department Ex p. Fire Brigades Union* (HL, 1995) and *R v Home Secretary Ex p. Bentley* (HC 1994) where the court was willing to review the Home Secretary's exercise of the prerogative of mercy. As can be seen however in Ch.6 the courts will often consider the subject matter of the decision they are asked to review inappropriate for judicial intervention and therefore, non justiciable.

THE CABINET AND THE PRIME MINISTER

All major government decisions are taken by the Cabinet, a committee of senior government ministers. It is for the Cabinet to determine the policies to be submitted to Parliament, to determine the content and priorities of legislative proposals, and to ensure that the relevant policies are carried out.

By convention all members of the Cabinet are collectively responsible for decisions taken. While the matter is under discussion ministers can air their views but once the matter is decided all members of the Government, whether within the Cabinet or not, must support it. If they are unable to do this then they should resign as Michael Heseltine did during the Westland affair and Robin Cook over the invasion of Iraq. The force with which this convention is observed has varied with the political climate. Indeed it was formally suspended during the campaign prior to the referendum on continuing membership of the EU.

There are no rules prescribing the size of the Cabinet. It has varied this century from small war time cabinets where the ministers have had no departmental responsibilities, to cabinets consisting of more than 20 ministers representing all the main departments of state. Increasingly the Cabinet operates through a network of committees, the result being that ministers may be bound by decisions in which they have had little more than nominal participation. Under Prime Minister Blair, political commentators have noted that cabinet meetings have become increasingly brief and formal.

As with the Cabinet itself, the office of Prime Minister is one which is barely recognised in law. This century has seen a steady increase in the powers of the Prime Minister who is now in a very strong position.

(a) As leader of the party in power, he has been chosen by the electorate, has control over the party machinery and can normally rely on the strength of party loyalty to maintain his position. His public profile is higher than that of any other minister.

(b) As chairman of the Cabinet, he can to a large extent determine the nature of discussions within the Cabinet. No votes are customarily taken. Rather, the Prime Minister sums up the sense of the meeting. Matters can be referred to sub-committees and the agenda manipulated to ensure the desired result.

(c) As ultimate head of the civil service, the Prime Minister has powers over senior appointments and access to all information.

(d) The Cabinet Office, although technically providing a service for all members of the Cabinet, has grown into the Prime Minister's special source of assistance and information. This greatly strengthens the Prime Minister's ability to argue against proposals put forward by departmental ministers who are forced to rely almost entirely on the briefs prepared for them by their departmental civil servants. This has been supplemented in recent years by a substantial increase in the use of "special advisers".

(e) The Prime Minister is the source of much patronage. He appoints and dismisses government ministers and has at his disposal a wide selection of public appointments, honours, etc.

It is, however, wrong to think of the Prime Minister as having absolute power. However dominant, he must keep the support of his party both inside and outside Parliament. Ultimately his strength will depend on his personality, but as Rodney Brazier points out, when affairs go badly his authority will wane and if luck deserts him he may well be finished. The removal of Prime Minister Thatcher in 1990 following her failure to win conclusively in the first ballot of the leadership election, emphasises the Prime Minister's ultimate dependence on continued party support.

Government ministers and departments

The various tasks undertaken by Central Government are executed by government departments such as the Treasury, the Home Office and the Department for Education and Skills. The organisation and responsibilities of these vary from time to time. At the head of each is a government minister, normally assisted by several junior ministers. Each minister will have a Parliamentary Private Secretary. By convention these will all be members of Parliament although not necessarily from the House of Commons. There is no legal limit on the number of ministers but there is a limit on the number who can sit and vote in the Commons (House of Commons Disqualification Act 1975, s.2(1)), presently 95, and a limit to the number of ministerial salaries which can be paid (Ministerial and other Salaries Act 1975). Under the Ministerial and other Salaries Act 1997, ministerial salaries are linked to those of civil servants.

    The departments are staffed by professional civil servants, each one headed by a Permanent Secretary. Civil servants must serve whatever government is in power even if they are not in sympathy with that government's views. To ensure this impartiality there are stringent restrictions on the degree of political involvement permitted to civil servants.

Government Agencies

The 1988 report, "Improving Management in Government, the Next Steps", led to the establishment of a number of government agencies. The aim was to rationalise the bureaucracy and to introduce a more management-oriented system. These agencies now carry out many of the functions formerly performed by the various government departments. Operational matters are made the responsibility of the chief executive of each agency which is run by a management board. The Permanent Secretary to the Department carries out a monitoring function on behalf of the Secretary of State. The Permanent Secretary remains the principal adviser on policy matters.

Ministerial responsibility

By convention, ministers are responsible to Parliament for the conduct of their departments *(Carltona v Commissioner of Works* (CA, 1943))*. In practical terms this may mean:

(a) Ministers may be legally responsible for the acts and omissions of their department and Government Agencies.

(b) Ministers are accountable to Parliament which has the right to question the minister on any aspect of the work of the department, even regarding events prior to his taking office. The Ministerial Code (1997) reminds Ministers of their duty to give accurate and truthful information to Parliament and to be as open as possible in accordance with the Code of Practice on Access to Government Information (1997).

(c) The degree of personal responsibility depends on the circumstances. Herbert Morrison once argued that ministers were responsible for every stamp stuck on every envelope and that if faults occurred within a department, the minister was at fault in that he had failed to lay down adequate procedures and systems of control. The modern tendency is that the minister is not required to shelter a civil servant who has acted improperly, particularly if he has disobeyed instructions or failed to follow established procedures. The Home Secretary, David Blunkett, blamed his civil servants for giving him wrong advice when his scheme for performance related pay for teachers was declared illegal by the courts.

Conversely, in 1991, the Home Secretary, Kenneth Baker, was able to shelter behind his legal advisers when he failed to order compliance with a judicial order requiring the return of a Zairian teacher to this country following his application for judicial review, arguing in the House that he had followed legal advice. Legally, however, he was technically responsible, the court holding that he had acted in contempt of court (*M v Home Office* (HL, 1991)).

Ministers who feel personally to blame, will normally resign, as for example Lord Carrington as Foreign Secretary following the Argentinian invasion of the Falkland Islands and ministers such as John Profumo who were involved in personal scandals. Otherwise, if a minister is criticised, no clear pattern emerges as to whether he will resign. Largely this is a political question depending on a number of factors such as the government's strength and the need to relieve pressure on it. (See the resignation of Leon Brittan during the Westland affair). Yet, despite the Scott Report's conclusion that ministers had failed to keep Parliament informed on changes in arms export policy to Iraq, no resignations occurred.

Some would argue that the establishment of Government Agencies has made it easier for ministers to avoid taking responsibility for mistakes by seeking to blame the Chief Executive of an Agency. An example of this was Michael Howard's attempt to hold Derek Lewis, Chief Executive of the Prisons Agency responsible for a prison breakout at Parkhurst Prison. It is sometimes difficult in practice to separate broad policy from day to day activities.

THE AVAILABILITY OF OFFICIAL INFORMATION

The traditional attitude of government has been that official information should remain secret unless the government chooses to make it available. This has sometimes been justified on security grounds but often the argument has been that disclosure is not in the public interest, that "secrecy is at all times the condition in which the best men make the best decisions".

The series of legal actions initiated by the Government to suppress publication of the memoirs of a former intelligence agent, Peter Wright, indicates the lengths to which the Government will go to ensure confidentiality. In *AG v Guardian News-papers* (No. 2) (HL, 1988) it was accepted that the Crown had a right to attempt to restrain disclosure of confidential information relating to the operation of the security services but that they must establish that the disclosure was in some way damaging to the public interest. In view of the widespread publicity given to Peter Wright's book "Spycatcher" it was felt that such damage could not now be established and the injunction against publication was discharged.

Cabinet discussions

The courts have protected the secrecy of cabinet discussions by granting injunctions and by refusing applications for discovery of documents. In *Att-Gen v Jonathan Cape Ltd* (HC, 1976) the court held that it had the power to restrain publication of material relating to such discussions although the power was not then exercised.

In *Conway v Rimmer* (HL, 1968) the need for secrecy was justified because:

(a) it ensured full and frank discussion within the cabinet;
(b) it helped to preserve the convention of collective responsibility;
(c) it protected governments from ill-formed or captious criticism.

This is less than convincing and the suspicion exists that the true reason for secrecy is to protect governments against criticism.

It is interesting to contrast the attitude of the British courts with that of the American Supreme Court where, in the Pentagon Papers Case, an order to restrain publication of accounts of high level discussion about policy in Vietnam, was refused.

The Public Records Acts

The Public Records Acts 1958–67 protected cabinet documents and other government papers for 30 years, unless the Government chose to make them available. The period could be extended if continued secrecy was deemed to be in the public interest. The Freedom of Information Act 2000 replaces the largely discretionary regime for access to public records with a new statutory regime and provides enhanced access to records more than 30 years old.

The Official Secrets Acts 1911–89

The overwhelming climate of secrecy was encouraged and supported by the Official Secrets Acts 1911–20 which were used not simply to prevent disclosure of security information but to prevent the disclosure of all information which governments chose not to disclose whether or not there were any national security implications.

The whole emphasis of the first Act in 1889 was on espionage and treason. The aim of the 1911 Act was to strengthen the law against spying. Section 1 covers all forms of spying making it an offence if any person, for purposes prejudicial to the interest of the state:

(a) approaches, inspects . . . enters any prohibited place; or
(b) makes any sketch, plan, model or note which . . . might be useful to the enemy; or
(c) obtains or communicates to any other person any information . . . calculated or intended to be, or which might be useful to the enemy.

In *Chandler v DPP* (HL, 1964) members of a group supporting nuclear disarmament were convicted under s.1 following an incident where they entered an RAF base and attempted to obstruct its use. This sabotage was held to fall within the conduct prohibited by s.1. The House of Lords held that the question whether the conduct was prejudicial to the interests of the state was for the court and not for the jury.

Section 2 of the 1920 Act provided that communicating with a foreign agent is evidence of obtaining or attempting to obtain information calculated or intended to be useful to an enemy contrary to s.1 of the Act.

But s.2 of the 1911 Act went far beyond spying, making it an offence to disclose or receive official information. This was not confined to security information but encompassed any information which was not in the interests of the state to disclose. The courts made it very clear that they equated the interests of the state with the interests of the government then in power. (See McCowan J. in *R. v Ponting* (HC, 1985)).

This offered the temptation to government to use s.2 to protect itself against potentially damaging disclosures. For example in the "whistleblower" trials of Sarah Tisdall and Clive Ponting no matters of national security seemed to arise. Their disclosures were, however, likely to cause serious political embarrassment to the Government.

The Official Secrets Act 1989, which repealed s.2 of the 1911 Act, is designed to protect more limited classes of official information. Section 1(1) makes it an offence for any member or former member of the security and intelligence services to disclose information relating to, or in support of, these services. Where the disclosure is by a crown servant or contractor, only those disclosures which are damaging to the public interest are criminalised. No such public interest defence is available to members of the security services charged under s.1(1). (See *R. v Shayler* (HL, 2001).)

In the case of disclosure of information on defence, international relations, crime, information resulting from unauthorised disclosures or entrusted in confidence by a crown servant, ss.2–5 make disclosure an offence if made without lawful authority and causing damage to the public interest. This is subject to the defence that the accused did not know the nature of the information or realise that its disclosure would be damaging.

The 1989 Act did not include a "public interest" defence for "whistleblowers" who felt that the public should be told certain information. The Public Interest Disclosure Act 1998, which provides employees who make disclosures about wrong-doings in the workplace with some protection against victimisation by employers, does not apply to the armed forces or members of the security services.

The "DA" notice system

In addition to the restrictions arising out of the Official Secrets Acts, the media is further restricted in what it can publish by a system of self-censorship known as the Defence Advisory Notice System. Much journalistic material is obtained from official sources "off the record". Because of the width of our official secrets legislation and the effect of laws on breach of confidence and contempt, the use of such information may constitute a breach of the law. Editors require some guidance as to whether action is likely to follow a particular disclosure.

This informal guidance is given by the Defence, Press and Broadcasting Advisory Committee which is composed of civil servants and representatives of the media. It issues "Defence Advisory" notices advising that those matters listed should not be published as they are required to remain secret for security reasons. Categories of information presently covered include information about nuclear weapons installations, the British Intelligence Services and highly classified military information. Editors can submit individual stories to the committee for guidance. It should be noted that any clearance is purely informal and does not give any immunity from prosecution. There have been occasions where, despite clearance being given by the Committee, the Government has sought an injunction restraining publication. Conversely, publication in breach of a "DA" notice is not, of itself, a criminal offence although the likelihood is that it will fall within the ambit of the legislation.

Freedom of information

Unless information about the workings of government is freely available, it is extremely difficult to call the government to account for its actions. There was a long campaign to change the climate of secrecy in British Government culminating in the Freedom of Information Act 2000.

An informal attempt to provide more official information was begun in 1977 when following the "Croham Directive" there was encouragement to government departments to make available background material relating to policy studies and reports. However, the effect of this was negligible and as it proved to be an expensive exercise, it was an early casualty of government spending cuts.

A 1993 White Paper on Open Government approved greater openness and a Code of Practice on Access to Government Information was introduced. There was not, however, a legal right to obtain the information. The Freedom of Information Act was passed in 2000 and will be fully implemented by 2005. This introduces a general right of access to information held by a wide range of public authorities listed in Sch.1 of the Act such as local and national government departments, schools, universities and hospitals, subject to certain conditions and exemptions. These exemptions, laid out in Pt II of the Act include security information, defence matters including anything relating to the capability and effectiveness of the armed forces, criminal proceedings and information whose disclosure is likely to prejudice this country's economic interests.

Where information is exempted from disclosure there is normally a requirement for the government or other public authority to explain why the need for secrecy outweighs the public interest in disclosure. Under s.19 public authorities must establish schemes which provide the public with effective access to information. The operation of the Act is policed by the Information Commissioner who must approve all disclosure schemes and who enforces the rights of access created by the Act. The Act is supplemented by new Codes of Practice, which provide guidance on specific issues. Any request for information must be made in writing and the authority in question is entitled to charge a fee for providing the information.

Critics have argued that the legislation is defective in a number of ways. The list of exemptions is extremely wide. It is not always easy to see how these can be justified in the public interest. The Act does not create a right to obtain the documents themselves only the information contained within them.

3. PARLIAMENT

THE COMPOSITION OF PARLIAMENT

Parliament consists of three elements:

(a) The Monarch. The Monarch gives the royal assent to legislation. The role is now essentially formal.
(b) The House of Lords.
(c) The House of Commons.

The House of Lords

This is currently a non-elected chamber. At the time of writing it comprises:
The Lords Temporal.

(a) 92 Hereditary Peers and Peeresses in their own right (The House of Lords Act 1999 removed the right of all other Hereditary peers to sit and vote. Those remaining were elected by their peers).
(b) Life Peers appointed under the Life Peerages Act 1958 (458).

(c) Lords of Appeal in Ordinary (The Law Lords) (30).

The Lords Spiritual.

26 Bishops of the Church of England, viz: Archbishops of Canterbury and York, the Bishops of London, Durham and Winchester and 21 other Bishops in order of seniority of appointment. They sit only so long as they continue to hold episcopal office.

In 1999 the Labour Government began a process of reform of the House but has had considerable difficulty in obtaining agreement to complete the changes (see below).

Disqualification for membership of House of Lords

(a) Aliens.
(b) Persons under 21.
(c) Undischarged bankrupts.
(d) Persons convicted of Treason—until sentence completed or pardon granted—Forfeiture Act 1870.
(e) Members expelled by the House unless pardoned.

The House of Commons

There are 659 MPs elected on a constituency basis by those entitled to vote by virtue of the Representation of the People Act 1983–2000. All Commonwealth citizens and citizens of the Republic of Ireland are entitled to vote if they are 18, are registered on the parliamentary register for that constituency on the qualifying date, and are not subject to any legal incapacity. Those compulsorily detained under the Mental Health Acts are disqualified as are persons convicted of certain corrupt or illegal practices at elections. Convicted criminals in penal institutions have traditionally been disenfranchised but in *Hirst v UK* (ECHR, 2004) it was held that a blanket ban on all prisoners irrespective of the offence or length of sentence, was in breach of the ECHR. The 2000 Act allows people who have no fixed residence to register by allowing them to make a declaration of local connection.

Elections for the Westminster Parliament are conducted by virtue of the "first past the post system", that is the candidate with the largest number of votes in a constituency is returned.

Disqualification for membership of the House of Commons

(a) Aliens. (Note—citizens of the Republic of Ireland are not barred.)

(b) Persons under 21.

(c) Persons of "unsound mind"—Mental Health Act 1983, s.141.

(d) Bankrupts until discharged—Insolvency Act 1986, s.427.

(e) Persons guilty of corrupt or illegal practices at elections. The extent of the disqualification depends on the precise offence—Representation of the People Act 1983, Pt III.

(f) Persons guilty of treasonuntil sentence completed or pardon granted.

(g) A person convicted of an offence and sentenced to a term of imprisonment for more than one year—Representation of the People Act 1981. This covers imprisonment in the United Kingdom or the Republic of Ireland.

(h) Those disqualified under the House of Commons Disqualification Act 1975 as holding "an office or place of profit under the Crown" (see updated Schedule, 1990).

This includes:

(i) Most major judicial offices (but not magistrates).

(ii) Civil servants, members of the armed forces and the police.

(iii) Membership of any legislature outside the Commonwealth, Euro MPs, members of the Scottish Parliament and the Welsh Assembly are not, however, disqualified.

(iv) Member of various boards, administrative bodies, chairmen of many public authorities.

(v) Under s.4 of the Act, the holders of certain specified offices of profit are disqualified, for example the Steward of the Chiltern Hundreds.

An MP who wishes to "resign" his seat must apply for one of the above offices of profit and thereby disqualify himself from sitting.

The former disqualification of clergy of the established church from membership of the Commons was removed by the House of Commons (Removal of Disqualification) Act 2001. Hereditary peers, apart from those still sitting in the House of Lords, are now no longer disqualified (House of Lords Act 1999).

DEVOLUTION OF GOVERNMENT

The Scotland Act 1998

This Act established a Scottish Parliament in Edinburgh. There are 129 members, 73 of whom are elected under a simple majority system and the remainder by proportional representation using the additional member system. Section 28 authorises the parliament to make laws known as Acts of the Scottish Parliament. The Scottish Parliament's legislative competence is however limited by s.29 which reserves certain matters for the Westminster Parliament. These are listed in Sch.5 and include foreign affairs, defence of the realm and many financial and economic matters. Under s.29(20(d)) a provision is outside the competence of the Parliament if it is incompatible with rights under the ECHR or with Community law. The Act does not preclude the Westminster Parliament from continuing to legislate for Scotland.

Money is allocated to Scotland by means of a block grant. Part IV of the Act gives the Parliament a tax-varying power of up to three pence in the pound.

The Act created a Scottish Executive consisting of a First Minister and Ministers drawn from the Members of the Scottish Parliament.

Government of Wales Act 1998

This set up the National Assembly for Wales. This does not have the legislative powers of the Scottish Parliament but rather carries out many administrative functions formerly exercised by the Secretary of State for Wales. Such powers are transferred to the Assembly by means of Orders in Council and include agriculture, education and economic development. It has no power to vary the rate of income tax. As with the Scottish Parliament the members are elected by a mixed system, 40 members on a first past the post constituency basis and a further 20 elected using the additional member form of proportional representation. The Leader of the Assembly is elected by that body and heads an Executive Committee.

Thus the Westminster Parliament continues to legislate for Wales and the Secretary of State for Wales continues to represent Welsh interests in the Cabinet. Under s.31 the Secretary of State for Wales is required, at the beginning of each session of Parliament to consult with the Assembly on aspects of the legislative programme which affect Wales.

The Northern Ireland Act 1998

Following the Good Friday Agreement in 1998 an elected Assembly was established consisting of 108 members representing 18 constituencies elected by means of the single transferable vote system. Section 1 of the Act declares that Northern Ireland in its entirety remains part of the United Kingdom and shall not cease to be so without the consent of a majority of the people of Northern Ireland. The Assembly was given the power to make laws to be known as Acts and the legislative competence of the Assembly was defined in s.5. As with the Scottish Parliament, certain matters are reserved for the Westminster Parliament. These include matters relating to defence and the crown. Part III of the Act established the posts of First Minister and deputy First Minister and empowered them to determine, subject to limitations on the overall number, the number of ministerial offices to be held by Northern Ireland Ministers and their functions. One aspect of the Belfast agreement was a power sharing arrangement among the major parties. The Assembly was suspended from midnight on October 14, 2002. Elections to the Northern Ireland Assembly were held on November 26, 2003. The Secretary of State has assumed responsibility for the direction of the Northern Ireland Departments.

THE WORK OF PARLIAMENT

The passage of legislation

Origins of legislation

At the beginning of each parliamentary session, the Monarch opens Parliament with a speech from the throne which outlines the Government's main proposals for the session. The programme will have been carefully considered by the Cabinet which decides on a timetable for the introduction of legislation. The details of this task are entrusted to the Future Legislation Committee of the Cabinet which has to cope with a flood of requests from the various Departments of State who all wish to have their proposals included.

The preparation of legislation is often a lengthy process. The content and policy of the Bill must be approved by the appropriate Cabinet committee and then by the full Cabinet. Reform may sometimes be preceded by Green or White Papers allowing prelegislative consultation in Parliament. Consultation will also take place with various interest groups. By the end of this prelegislative stage the main content of the Bill is effectively settled although further negotiations between the various interested parties continue throughout the passage through Parliament.

Responsibility for drafting the Bill is with the Parliamentary Draftsmen, officially known as Parliamentary Counsel to the Treasury. Their draft is scrutinised by the Legislation Committee of the Cabinet. The Law Officers are also likely to examine the Bill to consider such matters as the proper legal wording and the practicalities of implementation.

The Joint Committee on Human Rights

Every public Bill is now examined by the Joint Committee on Human Rights to determine whether it is convention compliant. It reports back to both Houses. The Government must, by the second reading stage, indicate whether the Bill is or is not compatible with the convention (s.19, HRA). The Human Rights Act does not, of course, prevent Parliament passing legislation which conflicts with our obligations under the ECHR but any non-compliance must be clearly indicated by the relevant minister.

Procedure for the passing of a Public Bill introduced by the Government into the House of Commons

1. First Reading. A purely formal stage.

The title of the Bill is read out, an order is made for the Bill to be published and a date fixed for the second reading.

2. Second Reading.

The principles of the Bill are discussed on the floor of the House. The Bill is voted on.

3. Committee Stage.

A detailed clause by clause analysis of the Bill by a standing committee of between 16–50 MPs. Detailed amendments are considered.

4. Report Stage.

The Bill is reported back to the whole House as amended. Further amendments, usually government sponsored, can be made at this stage.

5. Third Reading.

Once again the whole House considers the principles behind the legislation. Only verbal amendments can be made and any debate must be supported by at least six members.

Once a Bill has passed its Commons' stage it goes up to the House of Lords where the same process is repeated, except that the Committee stage is taken on the floor of the House. If the Bill is amended in the House of Lords, these amendments must be considered by the Commons. Often these amendments are tabled by the Government and so there is no problem in ensuring that the Commons will approve them. If, however, the amendments are rejected by the Commons, the Lords must decide whether to persist with these. If no agreement is reached before the end of the Session, the Bill will fail. The Government must then decide whether to reintroduce the measure in the following session and invoke the provisions of the Parliament Acts 1911–49.

Once the Bill is passed by both Houses it receives the Royal Assent. This is purely formal.

Variations on this procedure

1. Bills may start life in either House. The Government must try to arrange its business to ensure that the Commons does not have all its work at the beginning of the session and the House of Lords has all its work at the end. Generally less controversial Bills, *e.g.* technical legal Bills are selected to start life in the Lords, high profile political Bills in the Commons. As the House of Commons has sole responsibility for financial matters, it has to carry the burden of the work on financial Bills.

2. Some Bills have their Second Reading Stage in Committee. This is on the motion of a minister but can be prevented if 20 members object. This procedure was introduced in an attempt to save time on the floor of the House and is used for unopposed and non-controversial legislation. If the Second Reading is in Committee, the Report Stage will also be in Committee.

3. Some Bills have their committee stage on the floor of the House in the Commons. This procedure can be used for:
   (a) non-controversial Bills where the committee stage would be purely formal;
   (b) Bills of major constitutional importance where all members wish to be involved at every stage;

(c) Bills passed in an emergency;
(d) major clauses of Finance Bills.

In these cases Committee and Report Stages will be combined.

Effectiveness of parliamentary scrutiny of legislation

It has been argued that the present procedure for the passage of legislation does not provide effective scrutiny, that Parliament simply legitimises that which the Government has decreed. The following factors might indicate that scrutiny is ineffective.

1. The Government has a majority in the Commons and can normally force its measures through relying on such factors as the "whip system" and party loyalty.
2. The Government has control over the Parliamentary timetable and can curtail discussion and bring matters to a vote by the use of various procedural devices such as the "closure". Even in Committee there is no guarantee that every clause will be examined in detail. If a voluntary timetable cannot be agreed then the Government can "guillotine" proceedings.
3. Legislation has increased in volume and complexity over the years. MPs may lack the necessary expertise to scrutinise it effectively and may lack the necessary independent information.
4. There is a basic conflict between the need for technical scrutiny of legislation and the political need to oppose the legislation, to make it unworkable rather than improve it. As has been pointed out "the purpose of many opposition amendments is not to make the Bill more generally acceptable but to make the Government less generally acceptable."
5. The power of the House of Lords to amend legislation is limited by the Parliament Acts 1911–49.
   (a) There is no effective power to delay or veto a money Bill. This is a Bill certified by the Speaker as containing only provisions relating to the imposition, repeal or regulation of taxation, the imposition or variation of charges on the consolidated fund, etc., supply, the appropriation, receipt, custody, issue or audit of accounts of public money, the raising or guarantee of any loan or the repayment thereof, or subordinate

matters incidental to any of the above topics. The Speaker's certificate is conclusive.

(b) In the case of other public Bills (excluding a Bill to extend the life of Parliament) the House of Lords has no power of veto, only a power of delay. If a Bill is passed by the Commons in two successive sessions having been rejected by the Lords, it can be presented for the Royal Assent provided that one year has elapsed between the date of its second reading in the Commons in the first session and the date of its passing by the Commons in the second session. A rare example of the Parliament Acts being invoked occurred during the passage of the War Crimes Act 1991.

Yet Bills are considerably amended during their passage through Parliament. New clauses may be added. Concessions will be made. Parliamentary scrutiny is still important:

(a) It ensures the measure is publicised allowing opinion outside Parliament to make itself felt.

(b) The Government may be able to ignore the opposition but it cannot afford to ignore its own supporters. Backbench revolts are not unknown and many government sponsored amendments represent concessions made by Government to its own supporters.

(c) Establishment of Departmental Select Committees has increased the flow of independent information to MPs and increased specialist knowledge amongst backbenchers enabling them to scrutinise legislation more effectively.

(d) Party ties are less strong in committee and defeats do occur for the Government. It may then be a difficult political task to reverse these defeats on the floor of the House.

(e) If the House of Lords exercises its power of delay it ensures maximum publicity for the measure in question. Amendments are sometimes accepted by the Government against its better judgment to prevent disruption of the Parliamentary timetable.

It had been said in the past that there was a convention that the House of Lords would not pass amendments calculated to alter the kernel of a Bill approved by the Commons, but in recent years amendments have gone much further than altering the fine details of the Bill. Although it has been traditionally assumed that Labour Governments are more susceptible to defeat in the Lords than Conservative administrations, Brazier concludes that the Lords have been surprisingly even-handed in dealing out legislative defeats.

The Select Committee on the modernisation of the House of Commons has produced several reports recommending changes to enable Parliament to deal with more legislation, such as special standing committees, ad hoc commmmittees and pre-legislative committees. These are sometimes especially established, sometimes in conjunction with a House of Lords. Sometimes the work is undertaken by the relevant departmental select committee. The use of such committees is an excellent way of involving experts in the scrutiny of legislation.

Private Members' Bills

Backbenchers can introduce Bills in the following circumstances:

1. By being successful in the Ballot.
2. Under the 10-Minute Rule.
3. Under Standing Order 57.

On average 10-12 Private Members' Bills become law each session. These are mainly Ballot Bills.

Ballot Bills.   At a ballot at the beginning of each session, 20 names are drawn out of the hat by the Deputy Speaker. Those members, in order, have an opportunity to introduce their Bills before the House. Six Fridays are set aside in each session for the passage of such Bills although the Government can give extra time to measures it supports to ensure success.

The subjects chosen are wide ranging. A number of important social reforms have resulted from Ballot Bills such as abortion and divorce law reform. The only restriction is that the main purpose of the Bill must not be public expenditure. If some incidental expenditure is involved, the member must persuade a minister to move a financial resolution.

The procedure is identical to that of any other public Bill. Responsibility for drafting the Bill is borne by the Member although drafting assistance is given to any member whose Bill appears to have a chance of becoming law.

Not all Ballot Bills will be successful. As well as shortage of time, the Bill can be defeated on a vote or it can be talked out. It may be impossible to force a division as the support of 100 MPs is needed for the closure. It may also be difficult to maintain a quorum (40).

10-Minute-Rule Bills. Under Standing Order 23 on Tuesdays and Wednesdays, one member, selected by the Speaker on a first come, first served basis, has 10 minutes in which to outline his proposal for legislation. One speech in reply is permitted and the question is then put. It is extremely unlikely that legislation will result from this. Indeed the member will not have a draft Bill. The main purpose of this procedure is not to initiate legislation but to generate publicity for a particular issue or to test the water to see if there is support for legislation in the future. Even if a "Bill" succeeds at this stage, there is no further time allocated for the remaining stages and so, unless the Government gives up some of its time, the Bill will not proceed further. A report by the Select Committee on Procedure criticised the abuse of this process for publicity purposes and recommended that the text of any Bill proposed should be first lodged with the Public Bill Office. No action has been taken on this.

Standing Order 57. Under Standing Order 57 a member may present a Bill without obtaining leave from the House. This allows a member to take advantage of any gap in the Parliamentary timetable (these are rare) and present a measure. Only fairly simple, non-controversial Bills are likely to succeed by this method.

Delegated legislation Not all legislation is made directly by Parliament. Government ministers, local authorities and other public bodies have been given the power by statute to make subordinate legislation. This may be in the form of statutory instruments and orders, byelaws, regulations and orders in council.

The most important type of delegated legislation made by a minister is a statutory instrument. This is defined and regulated by The Statutory Instruments Act 1946.

Delegated legislation made by a minister acting under statutory authority which does not fall within this definition, is known as a statutory order. There is no more precise definition as it is simply a residual category. Statutory orders are not regulated by the 1946 Act.

Uses of delegated legislation

Delegated legislation is used mainly to add detail to primary legislation which may lay down the general principles although matters of considerable importance are sometimes dealt with in this way.

The use of delegated legislation saves Parliamentary time:

(a) Parliament can concentrate on the principles and ignore the details which can be worked out elsewhere.
(b) If the law requires updating this can be done without taking up time on the floor of the House.

It can also be said that the use of delegated legislation is desirable:

(a) It allows a certain flexibility in the law. It enables the minister, for example, to bring sections of an act into effect as and when required. It allows for regional variations, *e.g.* imposing restrictions on the movement of livestock during the foot and mouth outbreak. It even allows for a degree of experimentation in that the delegated legislation can be used to alter provisions in the parent Act.
(b) It facilitates full consultation with experts. Consideration of detailed, technical legislation in the contentious atmosphere of the floor of the House cannot be desirable.

But it does have its dangers, particularly when used to effect changes of substance. Then it can be argued that too much power is being concentrated in the hands of the minister. The procedure is much less public than that for the passage of Acts of Parliament. Clearly it is essential that, to prevent abuse, there is adequate control.

Control over delegated legislation

The enabling Act. The law-making power which Parliament intends to delegate should be expressed in clear and unambiguous language. The grant of wide discretionary powers makes it much more difficult to control the exercise of these powers by means of the doctrine of *ultra vires*. The enabling Act also determines the form in which the power is to be exercised. Greater control will be achieved by providing that the power is to be exercised by way of statutory instrument. It will then be regulated by the Statutory Instruments Act 1946 and will, if laid before Parliament, be subject to the scrutiny of the Joint Committee on Delegated Legislation.

Laying before Parliament. The enabling Act can provide that the instrument is to be laid before either or both Houses of Parliament. Various types of laying procedures are used:

(a) Greatest control is achieved by making the order subject to an affirmative resolution. This means the instrument will not come into effect until approved by Parliament in accordance with the laying requirement. Such instruments are automatically referred to a standing committee unless the House orders otherwise but the Government will have a majority in the committee and can normally force its measures through.

(b) Where an order is subject to a negative resolution it must be laid before Parliament (usually for 40 days) during which time a member can move a prayer to annul it. The order may come into effect as soon as it is signed by the relevant minister. If annulled it will simply cease being law. Attempts to annul such orders are rarely successful. Prayers must be moved at the end of the day's business, an unpopular time. Time for discussion is severely limited. The Government will normally have a majority and even if defeated, can reintroduce the measure and pressurise its supporters to defeat the motion. The order cannot be amended, simply withdrawn.

(c) Other forms of laying procedure are laying for information only and laying in draft.

Section 4 of the Statutory Instruments Act 1946 says that where a statutory instrument is required to be laid before Parliament then it shall be laid before the instrument comes into operation. This is subject to the proviso that where it is essential that an instrument comes into effect immediately, it can be brought into effect before it is laid, but that the Speaker and/or Lord Chancellor should be informed of this and the reason for it. In *R*.

v Sheer Metalcraft (HC, 1954) Streatfield J. said that a statutory instrument was complete "when made and laid." Together with s.4 this suggests that laying is a mandatory procedural requirement. However, *R. v Secretary of State for the Environment, Ex p. Leicester CC* (HC, 1985) said that where an order had to be laid before Parliament, laying before the House of Commons was sufficient as there had been substantial compliance with the procedural requirements.

Publication.   One difficulty in ensuring adequate scrutiny of delegated legislation is that not all delegated legislation need be published. In the case of statutory orders, any specific requirements as to publication must be stated in the enabling act. Statutory instruments are regulated by s.2 of the Act and must be sent to the Queen's Printer, numbered and put on sale. Some statutory instruments are exempt from this requirement by virtue of the Statutory Instruments Regulations 1947. This exempts instruments of a local or temporary nature, bulky Schedules and instruments which, in the opinion of the minister, it is not in the public interest to publish. Failure to comply with s.2 does not render the order invalid (Sheer Metalcraft, above).

It should, however, be noted, that s.3(2) of the Act provides a limited defence in the case of a person charged with an offence under an unpublished statutory instrument. In any proceedings it shall be a defence for the accused to prove that, at the date of the alleged contravention, the instrument had not been issued by Her Majesty's Stationery Office. It is then up to the minister to defeat the defence by proving that he had taken reasonable steps to bring the purport of the instrument to the notice of the public or of persons likely to be affected by it, or of the person charged. It is unlikely that this defence will be available in the case of every unpublished statutory instrument. The wording of s.3(2) appears to confine it to instruments which should have been published but, in fact, were not. This would exclude instruments exempted by the minister under the 1947 regulations and other types of delegated legislation. How strictly the section is to be construed remains in some doubt.

Scrutiny by Parliamentary Committee.

The Joint Committee on Statutory Instruments, which comprises seven members from each House plus a chairman drawn from the Opposition benches in the Commons, can examine all general statutory instruments and all other statutory orders subject to the affirmative procedure or special procedure orders. It is not concerned with the merits of the instruments but rather with whether the special attention of the House should be drawn to the legislation in that it:

(a) imposes a tax or fee on the public or a charge on the public revenue;
(b) is made pursuant of an enactment containing specific provisions excluding it from challenge in the courts;
(c) purports to have retrospective effect when there is no express authority in the enabling statute;
(d) has been unduly delayed in publication or laying before Parliament;
(e) has come into operation before being laid before Parliament and there has been unjustifiable delay in informing the Speaker;
(f) is of doubtful *vires* or makes some unusual or unexpected use of the powers conferred by the enabling statute;
(g) calls for any special reason of form or content, for elucidation;
(h) is defective in its drafting.

The Committee can consider only a fraction of the instruments laid before Parliament. Even when the Committee draws special attention to an instrument, no special Parliamentary notice need be taken. Indeed, by the time the Committee has reported, the instrument in question may have been dealt with.

Scrutiny by the Courts. The courts may be asked to consider whether delegated legislation is *ultra vires* the enabling Act. (See Ch.6). In interpreting the width of the power to make delegated legislation, the courts will apply certain presumptions, *e.g.* that there is no power to impose a tax unless stated expressly (*Att-Gen v Wilts United Dairies* (CA, 1921)); that there is no power to oust the citizen's right of access to the courts (*Chester v Bateson* (HC, 1920)); that the regulation will not operate retrospectively.

Parliamentary scrutiny of the Executive

Not since the nineteenth century can it be said that Parliament has made policy directly. This function has long since passed to the Cabinet. Parliament can still influence policy making, acting during its formulation by way of various interest groups and committees and by general expression of opinion on the floor of the House.

Its impact is limited by the strength of the Government which generally can control its own supporters and rely on its majority in the Commons. It is, today, simply one of many interest groups attempting to influence the decision-making process.

Parliament has, however, attempted to cling tenaciously to its role in the scrutiny of the implementation of that policy. After all, constitutionally, ministers are answerable to Parliament for the conduct of their departments. There are a number of opportunities in the Parliamentary year to examine the Government's record.

Debates

The Opposition parties have 20 days in each session in which they can select the topic for debate. Formerly this time was known as "Supply Days" and was used to discuss the grant of supply to the Crown but it has long ceased to be confined to discussion of government spending and is instead used to criticise all aspects of government policy. The Government itself provides time to debate such matters as the armed services and the EU, topics traditionally debated during supply days.

Emergency Debates are allowed at the discretion of the Speaker under Standing Order 24 if he considers that an application relates to "a specific and important matter that should have urgent consideration." The application must be supported by 40 members. There is reluctance to allow such debates in view of the considerable disruption caused to the Parliamentary timetable. There are, on average, two a year.

Certain opportunities are given to backbenchers to choose the subject matter for debate. Examples are:

(a) Adjournment Debates—half hour debates at the end of each day's sitting. Members ballot for a right to choose a topic and speak. A government minister will reply.
(b) Ten Fridays and four half days are given for private members' motions.
(c) Adjournment Debates following the passage of the Consolidated Fund and Appropriation Bills.

Apart from Emergency Debates which, because of their rarity will command widespread coverage in the media, such debates have limited value. The outcome is rarely in doubt. The opposition of the Opposition can be taken for granted. More important will be dissent shown during the debates by the Government's own supporters.

Since 1999 debates have also been held in Westminster Hall. These have tended to deal with constituency matters and other issues such as select committee reports which would be unlikely to be debated because of lack of time.

Parliamentary questions

Ministers are questioned in the House on a rota basis for 45 to 55 minutes on Mondays to Thursdays. The Prime Minister now only faces questions once a week on Wednesdays. Members can give no more than 10 days notice of a question and the questions are listed in the order in which they are tabled.

According to Erskine May the purpose is to obtain information, to press for action. It now appears that question time is used for the following purposes:

(a) To embarrass the Government by raising a sensitive issue.
(b) To publicise a particular matter, either nationally or in the MP's own constituency.
(c) To keep the Minister on his toes, to ensure he is au fait with the activities of his Department. This is done by asking an "open question" whose significance is not immediately apparent, and following it up with a supplementary. The Minister may be surprised into revealing more than he intended or reduced to admitting he does not know the answer, or even misleading the House. All these may do considerable damage to his reputation. Such open questions are widely used during questions to the Prime Minister.
(d) Some questions asked by the Government's own backbenchers are "planted" by the minister to enable him to release information.
(e) Prime Minister's Question Time is often used by the Opposition to make political points. It has variously been described as a "bear baiting session" and "a ritual exchange of non information."

Thus question time has limited use in obtaining the factual information necessary to enable MPs to scrutinise the activities of the Government. Ministers have warning of questions and need disclose no more information than they think fit and are obliged only to answer those matters which fall within their particular areas of responsibility. Thus as a formal method of scrutiny it has little value.

Written answers to questions.　Questions not dealt with on the floor of the House are answered in writing by the Minister and the answers published in Hansard. In addition, questions may be put down for written answer. Such questions are designed:

(a)　to obtain factual information;
(b)　to take up matters on behalf of constituents.

Although these may produce useful information, Ministers are skilled in revealing no more than is necessary.

One basic defect in these methods of scrutiny is that MPs must know the right questions to ask. As Government becomes more complex, it becomes increasingly difficult for MPs to have sufficient specialist knowledge to identify the key areas for investigation. Specialist knowledge, developed through membership of parliamentary committees, has proved invaluable here.

Parliamentary select committees

A more effective method of scrutiny than can be employed on the floor of the House is scrutiny by committees of MPs. Fourteen departmental select committees were established in 1979 to shadow the various departments of state. There are now 16 including Constitutional Affairs, Education and Skills and Culture, Media and Sport. Three Committees, Foreign Affairs, Home Affairs and Treasury and Civil Service have appointed sub-committees.

Membership.　Committees normally consist of 11 MPs, their membership reflecting party balance in the House. The chairmanships are shared between the main parties, the Government retaining some of the most sensitive, *e.g.* Defence, for itself. The committee members are appointed by the Committee of Selection. There is keen competition among backbenchers for places on the most prestigious committees and some complaints that the Committee of Selection which is essemtially controlled by the party whips, tends to appoint mainstream party members to the exclusion of formidable establishment critics. Government attempts to control the membership led, in 2001, to a backbench revolt.

Terms of reference. "To provide continuous and systematic scrutiny of the activities of the public service and to base that scrutiny on the subject areas within the responsibility of the individual Government Departments."

Specifically the committees have the following functions:

(a) To examine departmental estimates, to examine the policy objectives underlying these and consider whether the expenditure incurred would achieve these objectives in an economical manner. (The committees are supplied with proof copies of the estimates.)
(b) To examine all aspects of administration and policy relating to the department.
(c) To undertake special studies of areas of importance within the ambit of the department.
(d) To have a limited function in the examination of delegated legislation and European Secondary Legislation.

Increasingly committees try to monitor departmental performance against a host of targets.

Powers. The committees are empowered to take evidence from ministers, civil servants and outside experts and to call for the necessary papers and records. They will question regulators and the chairs of the various executive Agencies. The committee must, however, rely on Parliament to enforce these powers and this depends on the wishes of the Government of the day. The Select Committee on Defence investigating the "Westland Affair" wished to question civil service press officers and the Prime Minister's Press Secretary but the Government's refusal to allow them to testify effectively emasculated the committee. The committee accepted a compromise and took evidence from Sir Robert Armstrong and another senior civil servant. When the former Parliamentary Under Secretary of State for Health (Mrs Edwina Currie) had refused to give evidence to the Select Committee on Agriculture, the committee resolved to table a motion in the Commons forcing her attendance. She agreed to appear but her answers contributed little information. An argument about the production of Foreign Office telegrams regarding Sierra Leone was only partly resolved when the Foreign Secretary agreed to give oral evidence to the Foreign Affairs Select Committee and provide summaries.

Assessment. The committees have produced a considerable amount of valuable information which must assist MPs in their general task of scrutiny. The subjects studied have been wide ranging. They have not shied away from sensitive areas. In general it is felt that investigations into specific problems have been more valuable than wide ranging background investigations.

The reports have attracted considerable publicity. Clearly where a committee can issue a quick and reasoned comment on a topical subject it has the greatest impact. Committees are beginning to time their reports to correspond with appropriate business, such as legislation or a planned debate and this ensures greater coverage of their report. A major problem has been the delay before the government department in question produces any response to the report. The Committee on Procedure recommended a maximum of two months and this has now been accepted. MPs themselves appear enthusiastic and keen to participate. There have been no problems in staffing the committees and the membership has remained relatively static. This has enabled MPs to build up considerable expertise in their chosen fields. The Committees have all appointed specialist advisers. There is some evidence that committee members feel themselves less fettered by party ties in committee than on the floor of the House although there has been a tendency for party loyalty to reassert itself if the report is debated.

Yet the Committees cannot force ministers and civil servants to divulge information. The Government has made it clear that it believes a civil servant's responsibility is to his Minister, not to Parliament. This has led one MP to describe civil servants giving evidence to a committee as being "paralysed with caution."

Most commentators agree, for example, that the investigation by the Select Committee on Trade and Industry into the supply of a "supergun" to Iraq in breach of an embargo on arms sales, failed to uncover the truth. (Select Committee Report 1992). Similarly the investigation into the alleged "sexing up" of the dossier on the risk of Iraq mounting an attack on the West in

2003 did little to clarify the situation. The Hutton report was equally unsatisfactory in satisfying the public that there had been open and effective scrutiny of government action.

The Liason Committee has carried out a major review of the system over the last few years but there has been no change in the way members are appointed. Chairs are now paid an additional salary. More reports are debated in Westminster Hall but the proposal for regular debates on committee reports on the floor of the House has not been accepted.

Thus the new system may be an improvement but there is little evidence to support the view that the new committees exercise any real systematic control over the activities of government.

Control over financial matters

Constitutionally, Parliament has control over taxation and expenditure, although once again decisions are made by the Government. In recent years the Chancellor of the Exchequor has combined his statement on public expenditure with his Budget Speech. Those taxes imposed annually must be authorised by the Finance Act. Authority for levying taxation in the interim period is given by the Provisional Collection of Taxes Act 1968, a resolution of the House of Commons being insufficient authority (*Bowles v The Bank of England* (HC, 1913)).

Parliament's contribution to this process is confined to debates on the Budget and formal approval of government spending (*e.g.* by passing Consolidated Fund Acts and Annual Appropriation Acts which authorise payments out of the consolidated fund and the Finance Act which implements the Government's tax proposals).

There is little detailed Parliamentary control. Debates on the floor of the House are rarely concerned with matters of detail. The various departmental select committees looking at the estimates and the Public Accounts Committee looking at the accounts of what has been spent, can only scratch the surface. There is no Parliamentary control over Government borrowing.

The Comptroller and Auditor General, appointed by the Crown on a resolution of the House of Commons by virtue of s.1(1) of the National Audit Act 1983 has two major functions:

(a) to ensure that all money paid out of the government accounts has been properly authorised and is properly applied; and

(b) to examine the accounts of the various government departments.

Under the Audit Act 1983 this is more than a traditional audit. He is entitled to consider whether "objectives have been achieved in the most economical way." This has become known as "value for money" and "efficiency" auditing. He is not, however, entitled to question the merits of the policy itself.

He then reports to the Public Accounts Committee who will follow up a selection of his reports.

The National Audit Office, of which he is head, is also responsible for auditing the accounts of a wide range of bodies dependent on funds from Central Government such as the National Health Service and the Universities.

PARLIAMENTARY PRIVILEGE

To ensure that Members of Parliament and Parliament as a whole can carry out their functions effectively, they have certain privileges to safeguard them from outside interference.

Privilege of freedom of speech

To ensure an MP is free to carry out his Parliamentary duties and speak freely without fear of any legal repercussions, an MP has the privilege of free speech.

Absolute privilege

MPs have absolute privilege with regard to words spoken in the course of Parliamentary proceedings. (The Bill of Rights, Article 9.) Not only does this protect against actions of defamation but also against any criminal charges. Nor can they be found to be in contempt of court in relation to words spoken in the course of proceedings in Parliament. Perhaps the most serious incident was where several MPs deliberately identified an officer of the security services who had given evidence in court under the name Colonel B. The court had warned that any attempt to name the officer would be a contempt of court. No action could be taken by the court against the MPs.

In *Church of Scientology v Johnson Smith* (HC, 1972) an attempt was made to sue an MP claiming that he had slandered the Church of Scientology and its members. In order to succeed, it was necessary to show that the MP had spoken with malice. It was attempted to prove this by relying on a speech made by him in Parliament. The court held that these words could not be used as the words were absolutely privileged.

What are proceedings before Parliament?

It clearly covers debates, questions and everything said and done by a member both in committee and on the floor of the House. But as Erskine May points out, it does not follow that everything which is said and done within the confines of the chamber during a debate or other business forms part of a proceeding in Parliament. It would not, for example, cover a private conversation between two MPs. Nor does the geographical location of the speaker give automatic protection: *Rivilin v Bilainkin* (HC, 1953).

Difficulties have arisen as to whether letters written to Ministers by MPs in the course of their duties are covered by absolute privilege. This question arose in the Strauss case in 1958 when an MP, taking up a matter on behalf of a constituent, made certain allegations against the Electricity Board. The Chairman of the Board immediately issued a writ for libel. Strauss alleged that this was an infringement of his absolute privilege of free speech and as such was a contempt of Parliament.

The matter was referred to the Committee on Privileges which recommended that the matter was covered by absolute privilege but when this was debated by the whole House, it was accepted that writing to a Minister was not a proceeding before Parliament. Accordingly the House rejected the committee's recommendations and ruled that the issuing of the libel writ was not a contempt. In fact the writ was then withdrawn.

Parliament is not bound to follow this in the future. Indeed the view has sometimes been expressed that there is a clear advantage in keeping the scope of this privilege indefinite. Despite this there have been various Parliamentary attempts to define the phrase. In Session 1969–70 the Select Committee on Privileges recommended that it should cover:

(a) all things done or written in each House or in Committee for the purpose of business being transacted;
(b) all things done between members and officers, between members, and between members and ministers for the purpose of enabling any of these to carry out their functions.

A possible limitation to this is the suggestion that it would cover only those matters which had been before the House, or at least those coming before the House in the current Parliamentary session. (See *Rost v Edwards* (HC, 1990)).

Qualified privilege

An MP may rely on the defence of qualified privilege in regard to words spoken in the course of his duty as an MP. This means that he is protected against any action of defamation provided he speaks in good faith and without malice *(Beach v Freeson* (HC, 1972)), and provided there is a common interest between the parties.

In recent years MPs have made use of this privilege to make defamatory allegations. While Parliament itself can regulate such matters it has shown itself reluctant to do more than call on "the good sense of MPs not to abuse their privilege".

Following the case of *Prebble v Television New Zealand Ltd* (PC, 1995), the High Court halted a libel action by Neil Hamilton MP against the Guardian newspaper on the basis that much of the evidence could not be explored as it related to "proceedings in Parliament". The potential unfairness of this led Parliament to amend Art.9 of the Bill of Rights. The Defamation Act 1996 allows individuals to waive the rule which prevents evidence of proceedings in Parliament being considered by a court.

Reports of parliamentary proceedings

At common law no protection was given to those reporting speeches made in Parliament. The MP was absolutely privileged but the reporter and the publisher could face civil or criminal action *(Stockdale v Hansard* (HL, 1839), where libel damages were awarded against Hansard who had printed verbatim an author-ised House of Commons Report).

Protection is now given by the Parliamentary Papers Act 1840. Section 1 gives *absolute protection* against any civil or criminal action to anyone publishing papers printed by order of Parlia-ment. This will cover, for example, White Papers and Hansard, the daily journal of the House. If any proceedings based on such papers are initiated, these must be stayed on production of a certificate issued by the Speaker or the Lord Chancellor. Section 2 gives *absolute protection* to any copy of such paper. Section 3 only protects against actions of defamation in that it gives *qualified privilege* to extracts from any reports protected by ss.1

and 2. This means that such extracts are protected provided the defendant can show that they were published in good faith and without malice. (*Dingle v Associated Newspapers* (HC, 1960)). Reports of Parliamentary proceedings are also protected by the ordinary law of defamation in so far as they are fair and accurate unless the defamed person can prove malice (Defamation Act 1996). The basis of this protection is that publication is deemed to be for the benefit of the public. In *Cook v Alexander* (CA, 1973) qualified privilege was accorded to a "Parliamentary Sketch" which, although impressionistic and selective, was considered by the court to be sufficiently balanced as to be fair and reasonable. No special protection has been given to the broadcasting of the proceedings of the House but broadcasters can claim the protection given to any fair and accurate report under the 1996 Act.

Privilege of freedom from arrest

MPs have no privilege protecting them against an arrest on criminal charges but they are protected against arrest in connection with a civil matter while Parliament is in session and for 40 days before and after. This is of no real practical importance today.

Parliament's right to determine its own composition

1. The Commons has the right to fill casual vacancies by calling a by-election.
2. The Commons can determine the result of disputed elections. In practice this is now dealt with by an Election Court.
3. Parliament has the right to determine whether members are legally disqualified. In the Wedgwood Benn case in 1961 the House of Commons refused to allow Tony Benn to take his seat although he had been duly elected. He had succeeded to a peerage on the death of his father and was disqualified from sitting in the Commons. The disputed succession to the Barony of Moynihan was determined by the Committee of Privileges of the House of Lords, its report being accepted by the House in 1997.
4. The House may expel members whom it considers unfit to serve.

Parliament's right to regulate its own internal proceedings

Parliament is empowered to regulate its own internal proceedings. It may make standing orders to govern its procedures. The courts have always refused to consider whether these procedures have been complied with (*Pickin v British Rail Board* (HL, 1974)).

The privilege is much wider than procedural matters, covering every aspect of the internal functions of the House. In *R. v Graham-Campbell, Ex p. Herbert* (HC, 1935) the Court refused to investigate an alleged breach of the licensing laws by the "Kitchen Committee" of the House of Commons.

In *Bradlaugh v Gossett* (HC, 1884) Parliament expelled an MP who refused to take the oath of allegiance to the Crown under the Parliamentary Oaths Act 1866, on the ground that he was an atheist and the oath would be meaningless. At a by-election he was re-elected and indicated that he was now willing to take the requisite oath. Parliament resolved that he should be prevented, if necessary by force, from taking his seat. It was said that "the House of Commons is not subject to the control of the courts in the administration of that part of statute law which has relevance to its own internal proceedings." The court would not intervene.

Parliament's power to punish for contempt

The following have been held to be contempts of Parliament:

1. An attempt to interfere with a Member's freedom of action. In the *NUPE* Case (HC, 1976/77) the national conference of NUPE passed a resolution demanding that the union's executive withdraw union sponsorship from those MPs who supported their party's public expenditure cuts. The Committee of Privileges found this to be a contempt but no action was taken when the General Secretary of the Union gave assurances that sanctions would not be imposed on MPs. Other attempts to obstruct members in the execution of their duty such as bribery or threats have also constituted contempt.
2. Misconduct in the House or disobedience of the rules of the House, *e.g.* failure to co-operate with a Parliamentary Committee, disruptive behaviour in the House.
3. Misconduct by MPs in the House. When John Profumo was found to have lied to the House this was a contempt (*Profumo's Case 1962/63*). Corruption, taking bribes, failure to declare a conflict in interests have all constituted contempts. Recent concerns have related to the employ-

ment of MPs as consultants and lobbyists and the employment of ex-cabinet ministers in positions where use could
be made of their "inside knowledge". (See the Nolan
Report.)
4. Publication of materials reflecting on the proceedings of
the House and its members. Newspaper articles criticising
MPs have been held to be a contempt. (*Sunday People Case*
(HC, 1976/7)). Publication of false reports of Parliamentary proceedings and premature disclosure of committee
proceedings have both constituted contempt.

Thus contempt is wider than simply breach of any of Parliament's privileges but can consist of any conduct which interferes with the workings of Parliament or is likely to bring
Parliament or its members into disrepute. If an MP feels that a
contempt has occurred, he first complains to the Speaker who
considers whether a breach of privilege has *prima facie* occurred.
If so, the House has the opportunity to consider whether the
matter should be referred to the Committee on Standards and
Privileges.

Members can be suspended or expelled for contempt. The
House also has the power to admonish or issue a reprimand to
those in contempt. Journalists may be barred from the House for
a period of time. While the House has the power to imprison for
contempt, this was last used in 1880. The House has no power
to fine although this has been recommended.

Members financial interests

Following the Poulson scandal in the early 1970s where three
MPs had misused their position as MPs to promote Poulson's
business interests, the House set up a register of members'
interests to make public any business and other interests which
might influence their behaviour. A number of incidents in the
early 1990s culminating in the "cash for questions" affair led to
the establishment of the Nolan Committee into Standards in
Public Life. This, in turn, led to the establishment of the
Parliamentary Commissioner for Standards, a much more comprehensive register of members' interests, a reformed Committee of Standards and Privileges and a standing committee to
inquire into standards in public life. This latter committee has
considered, for example, the relationship between MPs and
lobbyists. The Parliamentary Commissioner for Standards has

carried out a number of investigations into the activities of MPs including certain business interests of the then junior minister Keith Vaz. The courts have refused to review the Commissioner's activities as they are concerned with matters within Parliament (*R. v Commissioner for Standards, Ex p. Al-Fayed* (CA, 1998)).

THE ROLE OF THE HOUSE OF LORDS

The role and composition of the House of Lords has been subject to considerable criticism.

1. Its composition. The inclusion of hereditary peers was criticised as inappropriate in that it drew on a narrow social class who were not representative of the country as a whole and were there simply by birth. The introduction of life peerages was partly designed to broaden the base of membership but life peers did not made as large a contribution to the work of the House as had been hoped. Too often life peerages have been used as a reward for political service. As noted above the majority of hereditary peers were removed by the House of Lords Act 1999.
2. It is not elected. It has been argued that it is wrong for such a body to impose even a limited check on the activities of an elected Government.
3. It has been criticised for political bias. It was alleged that there was an in-built conservative majority. The introduction of the life peerage system and the fact that peers can apply for leave of absence at the beginning of each session tended to redress this although those taking the Conservative Whip continued to constitute the largest single grouping. The last two Labour Governments have created a number of "working peers" in an attempt to redress the balance.

Yet it does perform a number of useful functions:
1. Legislative functions.
    (a) A number of Bills, mainly non-controversial, start life in the Lords.
    (b) The House does a considerable amount of scrutiny of complex and technical legislation. Many Government amendments are brought in the Lords to save time in the Commons.

(c) It bears the brunt of the examination of private Bills.

(d) It does valuable work in the scrutiny of delegated legislation including European secondary legislation. Not only does this save time in the Commons, it provides another type of less politically charged scrutiny by those who may have a wide range of expertise and experience.

2. Debating function. The House of Lords provides a useful forum for debating the great issues of the day.

3. Check on government. It is argued that in view of the impotence of the House of Commons and the flexibility of the British Constitution, it is necessary for there to be some check on the activities of Government. Although limited by the Parliament Acts and the convention of non-involvement in financial matters, the House of Lords is the only such check. The Lords can publicise matters and delay action for long enough to allow public opinion to make itself felt.

Reform of the House of Lords

Completing the reforms initiated in 1999 has proved to be extremely difficult.

Debate over the future of the House of Lords has centred around the following issues.

The need for a bicameral legislature

A considerable amount of work is done on legislation, including work on private bills, delegated legislation and legislation arising out of our EU obligations. As presently organised the House of Commons would not have time to do this. There are many examples of Bills proceeding to the Lords following limited scrutiny and considerable numbers of government amendments being brought in the Lords. It could be argued that what is needed is reform of the Commons to enable it to cope with the volume of work. There is, however, an argument that scrutiny and revision by a different chamber has value in bringing a different, less party political perspective.

A further justification for a second chamber is that it imposes a check on the House of Commons. We do not have a written constitution or a constitutional court to test the legitimacy of government action. In view of the government's usual tight control of the Commons, a second chamber may have value. But should the current one year delaying power be cut?

The composition of the second chamber

There are clear concerns about an Upper House consisting largely of Government nominees and any extension of Prime Ministerial powers of patronage. It would of course be possible to take the selection of life peers out of the hands of government and establish an independent commission. Other suggestions have included nomination by various interest groups. This would promote the inclusion of experts although one might question whether this would produce a group of people willing to take an overall view. Since 2000 all nominations have been scrutinized by an Advisory Committee.

Another alternative is an elected chamber. This would answer critics who point to the undemocratic nature of an appointed House. An obvious difficulty of having the same method of election for both Houses is that it would tend to produce a mirror image and devalue the role of the House of Lords as a check. If a different method was employed there would undoubtedly be arguments as to which House better represented the wishes of the people.

A combination of appointed and elected members is the favoured solution.

In February 2003 Parliament was asked to vote on various options ranging from a wholly elected House, a wholly appointed House and various proportions of each. It proved impossible to obtain agreement on any one option although the preferred option of the House of Commons was for a majority of elected members. It was decided not to proceed with reform at that stage. There followed a further consultation paper on House of Lords reform in September 2003. This set out a proposal for the removal of the remaining hereditary peers and the establishment of a new independent statutory Appointments Commission. Legislation was introduced but it became clear that the Bill was unlikely to succeed. The Government announced on March 18, 2004 that it was not proceeding with the legislation to enact the proposals of the consultation paper.

4. THE POLICE AND THE PUBLIC

THE INVESTIGATION OF OFFENCES

The police are entrusted with the power to investigate offences, yet, just because a person comes under suspicion of being involved in criminal activity, does not mean that he loses all rights to the freedom of his person. The law has to strike a balance between preserving and safeguarding the rights of individuals and giving the police the necessary powers to carry out these tasks effectively.

Section 6 of the Human Rights Act 1998 makes it unlawful for the police, as a public authority, to act in a way that is incompatible with a convention right. Thus the police, in investigating offences will, for example, have to act in accordance with Arts 5, 6 and 7 of the ECHR. Any restrictions on an individual's liberty must be framed with sufficient precision to allow the citizen to foresee the consequences of their actions and avoid the grant of arbitrary power.

The police have the right to ask anyone questions in the course of their duties but, although there may be a moral duty to help the police, there is no legal duty.

(a) There is no obligation to answer questions (*Rice v Connolly* (HL, 1966)). A person should not be forced to incriminate himself. It should be noted that, although a suspect is still able to choose to remain silent, in certain circumstances a failure to answer questions might have evidential consequences. Under s.34 of the Criminal Justice and Public Order Act 1994 where a suspect is being questioned under caution or is being charged with an offence, and fails to mention a fact which he subsequently relies on in his defence, the court may be allowed to draw an adverse inference from the suspect's silence, if it considers it to have been reasonable for the accused to have mentioned the fact when questioned or charged.

Under s.36 a similar inference may be drawn from a failure to provide an explanation where objects, substances or marks are found on a suspect or in the place the suspect was at the time of the offence. Before such an inference can be drawn, the requirements of s.36(b), (c) and (d) must be satisfied (See *R. v Argent* (CA, 1996)).

Silence on its own will not of itself, be sufficient evidence of guilt. The prosecution will always be required to produce other evidence;

(b) Failure to answer police questions does not, by itself, amount to obstruction of the police in the execution of their duty;

(c) If a person is voluntarily helping the police, that person is entitled to terminate the interview and leave at any time. If the police wish to detain him they must place him under arrest. Section 29 of the Police and Criminal Evidence Act 1984 (PACE) provides that he should be informed at once that he is under arrest if a decision is taken to prevent him leaving at will.

Power to stop and search

In the course of their duties the police may wish to search a suspect for evidence of an offence. This power has long been seen as a contentious area of police activity and a major cause of tension between minority groups and the police. The Stephen Lawrence Inquiry highlighted its negative effect on community relations and led to the Code of Practice on Stop and Search (Code A) being revised in an attempt to provide greater safeguards against any discriminatory use of the power. Statistics produced in 2004 show that black people are six times more likely to be stopped and searched than white. This has led to the Government establishing an action team to produce further guidance in the form of a stop and search manual.

Code A emphasises that the power must be used fairly and responsibly with respect for people being searched and without unlawful discrimination.

A police officer can only carry out a stop and search where there is a legal power to do so. The consent of the suspect is no longer enough. The only exception to this is where a search is carried out as a condition of entry, *e.g.* to sports events.

Under s.1 of PACE the police can stop and search:

(a) any person or vehicle;
(b) anything which is in or on a vehicle,

for stolen or prohibited articles or articles with blades or points as defined in s.139 of the Criminal Justice Act 1984, and may detain a person or vehicle in order to conduct such a search. Section 1(6) gives the power to seize such items.

A prohibited article includes:

(a) an offensive weapon;

(b) an article made for, or intended to be used for, burglary, theft, theft of a motor vehicle, obtaining property by deception.

The officer must have reasonable grounds for stop and search (s.1(3)). Whether such grounds exist will depend on the circumstances of each case but there must be some objective basis for it. Code of Practice A on Stop and Search, says that an officer will need to consider the nature of the article suspected of being carried in the context of other factors such as the time, place and behaviour of the person concerned or those with him. Reasonable suspicion may exist, for example, when information has been received such as a description of an article being carried.

Reasonable suspicion can never be supported on the basis of personal factors alone. For example a person's colour, age, hairstyle or manner of dress or the fact that he is known to have a previous conviction for possession of an unlawful article, cannot be used alone or in combination with each other as the sole basis on which to search that person. Nor may suspicion be founded on the basis of stereotyped images of certain persons or groups as more likely to be committing offences. Personal factors can, of course, be taken into account together with other, more objective factors. Thus reasonable suspicion should normally be linked to accurate intelligence.

The extent of the search

The Code envisages a minimal interference with a person's liberty. The suspect's co-operation must be sought and every effort made to avoid embarrassment. Under s.117 of PACE reasonable force may be used if necessary. Searches are restricted to superficial examination of outer clothing. Section 60AA of the Criminal Justice and Public Order Act 1994 allows the police to remove items such as masks which are being used to conceal the suspect's identity and the Terrorism Act 2000 does permit the removal of headgear and footwear in public. The thoroughness and extent of the search depends on what is suspected of being carried. So, for example, if the suspicion relates to an article slipped into a pocket, the power of search will relate only to that pocket. If a fuller search is deemed necessary, it must be done in a suitable place by an officer of the same sex and, unless the suspect consents to accompany the officer, he must first be arrested. As was noted above, in certain circumstances a failure to answer questions may have evidential consequences.

Location of search

The power can be exercised in any place to which the public has access whether on payment or not, excluding dwelling houses or other private premises such as private clubs. It covers streets, common areas of flats, such as stairs and walkways, pub car parks, etc. Note, however, the position relating to the yards and gardens of houses. The police cannot use stop and search powers there unless they are satisfied that the suspect does not reside there, or is there with the permission of the owner of the property. (Sections 1(4) and 1(5).)

Other powers

PACE does not encompass all existing stop and search powers. Other powers are given by such Acts as the Misuse of Drugs Act 1971 (permits the police to stop and search for controlled drugs anywhere). Under s.60 of the Criminal Justice and Public Order Act 1994, where it is reasonably believed that incidents involving serious violence may take place in a locality and it is expedient to use the powers given under the Act to prevent their occurrence an officer of the rank of Inspector or above may authorise special stop and search powers (See Ch.5). A uniformed officer may then search any person for offensive weapons. Under the Terrorism Act 2000 an officer of the rank of assistant chief constable or above may authorise stop and search powers in a specified locality for up to 28 days if he considers it expedient for the prevention of acts of terrorism. In *Gillan v Commissioner of Police for the Metropolis* (CA, 2004) it was confirmed that the order could cover the whole of a police area, in this case the whole Metropolitan Police District and that a rolling programme of 28 day authorizations was justified in the current situation. As with s.60 there is no need for the officer making the stop to have any level of suspicion against the person being stopped.

Safeguards

Before a search takes place

(a) The officer must identify himself (s.2(3)(a)). Failure to do so will invalidate the search. (*Osman v DPP* (1999));

(b) He must take reasonable steps to explain what he is looking for and the basis of his suspicion (s.2(3)(b)).

After the search

(a) He must normally make a record of the search there and then unless there are exceptional circumstances. This record should cover the ethnic group, identity of the suspect, object, grounds of search, place and time, date and results (s.3). This record should be made available to the suspect on request and is designed to facilitate any complaints of unjustifiable action by the police;

(b) If an unattended vehicle has been searched, a note should be left recording this fact and indicating the officer responsible (s.2(6)).

These requirements have become more stringent over the years and now apply to all searches.

Arrest

This is a fundamental step in the criminal process designed to ensure the person is available to answer charges before a court. It is not the only way in which a person can be brought before a court. In the case of less serious offences a person can be summonsed to appear.

Article 5 of the ECHR emphasises that arrest and detention must not be arbitrary. Cases such as *Murray v UK* (ECHR, 1994) emphasised that a "reasonable suspicion" test must be established. In *Castorina v CC of Surrey* (1988), the court said that while the arresting officer might not yet be in a position to prove anything, he must have some factual basis for his suspicion.

In *Hough v Chief Constable of Staffordshire* (CA, 2001) the arresting officer's suspicion came from information in the police national computer. This was, in fact, wrong. Despite this the court held that there was "reasonable suspicion".

The justification for the arrest

Arrest under warrant

Under s.1 of the Magistrates' Court Act 1980, a warrant for arrest may be issued by a magistrate on sworn information by the police. It must identify the suspect and the offence on which it is founded.

Summary power of arrest

In the following circumstances the police have the power to arrest without a warrant.

Arrestable offences

Section 24 provides for a power of summary arrest in respect of *arrestable offences* as defined in that section.

An arrestable offence is:

(1) an offence for which the sentence is fixed by law (murder, treason);

(2) an offence for which a person of 18 or over may be sentenced on first conviction to imprisonment for a term of five years (this covers common law and statutory offences);

(3) those offences listed in s.24(2), *e.g.* Theft Act 1968 (ss.12(1) and 25(1)). These do not meet the sentencing requirement but are nevertheless deemed to be arrestable offences.

Conspiring or attempting to commit such offences, inciting, aiding, abetting, counselling or procuring the commission of such offences may also be arrestable offences.

Some offences under s.24(2) already attracted a power of summary arrest under individual statutes. The effect of making them arrestable is that it gives the police certain powers of entry and search under ss.17 and 18 while investigating the offences in question.

The combined effect of these provisions is to give a power of summary arrest in the case of all the more serious offences and many of the most commonly committed offences, *e.g.* murder, manslaughter, the major offences against the person, offences under the Criminal Damage Act and almost all the Theft Act offences.

Section 26 repealed a number of existing statutory powers of summary arrest. Those retained are listed in Sch.2 and include powers under the Immigration Act 1971 and the Criminal Justice and Public Order Act 1994. As these are not arrestable offences the specific powers under PACE are not triggered.

The police and the citizen may arrest:

(a) Anyone who is in the act of committing an arrestable offence.
(b) Anyone whom he has reasonable grounds for suspecting to be committing such an offence.
(c) Anyone who has committed an arrestable offence or he has reasonable grounds for suspecting has committed an arrest able offence.

The police officer has additional powers of arrest:

(a) He can arrest where he has reasonable grounds for suspecting that an arrestable offence has been committed and he has reasonable grounds for suspecting the person to be guilty of the offence.
(b) He has a preventative power in that he can arrest anyone who is about to, or he has reasonable grounds to suspect is about to, commit an arrestable offence.

Non-arrestable offences—section 25

The police have a power of summary arrest in the case of non-arrestable offences, but only where service of a summons appears to the officer to be impracticable or inappropriate because any of the general arrest conditions noted below apply. These are:

(a) That the officer cannot discover the suspect's name or believes he has given a false name (*Nicholas v DPP* (HC, 1987)).
(b) That there is no satisfactory address for serving the summons.
(c) That the constable has reasonable grounds for believing that arrest is necessary to prevent the relevant person:
  (i) causing physical harm to himself or another;
  (ii) suffering physical injury;
  (iii) causing loss or damage to property;
  (iv) committing an offence against public decency;
  (v) causing an unlawful obstruction of the highway.
(d) That the constable has reasonable grounds for believing that an arrest is necessary, *e.g.* to protect a child.

It is important to note that an offence, however trivial, must have been suspected, in order to trigger these provisions.

To prevent a breach of the peace

At common law the police have long had the power to effect an arrest to prevent a breach of the peace. (*R. v Howell* (CA, 1981). In exceptional circumstances the police may even arrest a person who was not acting unlawfully as in *Bibby v Chief Constable of Essex* (CA, 2000), where a bailiff attempting to seize goods under a liability order was asked to leave premises by the police who were trying to calm the situation down. He refused and was arrested. The court found it justified in the circumstances as there was a real threat of a breach of the peace and the bailiff's conduct was unreasonable.

Formalities of arrest

The Act requires the person arrested to be informed that he is under arrest as soon as practicable even if the fact that he is under arrest is obvious (ss.28(1) and (2)).

He must also be told of the ground of the arrest at the time or as soon as is practicable thereafter (s.28(3) and *DPP v Hawkins* (HC, 1988)). In *Edwards v DPP* (HC, 1993) the fact that the police officer gave a wrong reason for the arrest, rendered the arrest invalid.

Section 28 enacts in statutory form the rule laid down in *Christie v Leachinsky* (HL, 1947) where Lord Simon said that the suspect was entitled to know on what charge or on suspicion of what crime he was seized. If the citizen is not so informed the police may be liable for false imprisonment unless, of course, the suspect makes this impossible by his conduct (*Lewis v Chief Constable of South Wales* (CA, 1990)). Lord Simon stressed that technical or precise language need not be used (See *Abbassy v Newman* (CA, 1989)). Section 28 varies the decision in *Leachinsky* in that Lord Simon said that if the facts were obvious, if, for example the suspect has been caught red handed, it was not necessary to inform him why he had been arrested. Section 28(4) now says that the person must be told the reason for the arrest even if the facts are obvious (*Nicholas v DPP* (HC, 1987)).

Arrest elsewhere than at a police station

Section 30 says that, on arrest a suspect should be taken to a police station as soon as practicable unless the investigation requires his presence elsewhere. This must normally be a designated station, that is one which has a custody officer and has the necessary facilities to cope with those detained following arrest. But, see *Vince and Another v Chief Constable of Dorset* (CA, 1992). He need not be taken to a designated police station if it is not anticipated he will be detained for more than six hours or where the arresting officer is without help.

Once the decision is taken to arrest a suspect he must not normally be interviewed about the offence except at a police station. This is to ensure the various protections noted below will apply. An interview is defined in Para.11 of Code C.

Search on arrest

Section 32 regulates searches where an arrest is made away from a police station. A constable has a right to search for a weapon if he has reasonable grounds for believing that the suspect might present a danger to himself or others, for example because he was acting violently or was drunk or suicidal. The suspect may also be searched for anything he could use to effect his escape and for evidence relating to any offence if there are reasonable grounds for suspecting that the items are in the suspect's possession.

Such a search must be relatively cursory. If a person is searched in public he cannot be required to remove anything other than his coat, jacket or gloves.

Following an arrest the police may search the premises where the suspect was immediately prior to or at the time of the arrest for evidence relating to that offence (s.32(2)(b)); *R. v Beckford* (CA, 1991)). If he has been arrested for an arrestable offence, there may also be a power to search his home under s.18.

Section 54 requires the custody officer to ascertain what property a detained person has with him. He is responsible for its safekeeping. To that end he is entitled to search him. Cash and items of value are kept for safekeeping. The detained person can retain his clothing and personal effects unless the custody officer considers that, in terms of s.54(4), he may use them to cause harm to himself or others, effect an escape, damage property or interfere with evidence.

Code C defines personal effects as those items which a person may lawfully need or use etc. not including cash or other items of value. (Para.4.3.)

Anything else can be seized. Intimate and Strip searches must be conducted in accordance with Annexe A to Code C.

Under s.54(6)A, there is a power to search a suspect in custody at any time to ascertain whether he has anything he could use for the purposes specified in s.54(4).

Intimate searches are regulated by s.55 and Annexe A of Code C.

QUESTIONING IN POLICE CUSTODY

The opportunity to question suspects in custody is clearly of crucial importance to the police. The suspect, however, is in a very vulnerable situation. The recognition in PACE of the power to detain suspects after arrest, but before charge is balanced by attempts to give some protection to the suspect. These arise from the imposition of maximum time limits for detention, periodic review of the need for such detention, the statutory rights of access to a solicitor and a Code of Practice on Detention and Questioning (Code C). The Custody Officer has a pivotal role in ensuring these rules are properly observed.

The Custody Officer

The Custody Officer is responsible for safeguarding the rights of suspects at the police station. Section 36(5) stresses his independence allowing only minimal involvement at an earlier stage of the investigation.

His main duties are:

(a) To determine if the suspect's detention is valid. If not he should be released with or without bail (s.34(1)).

(b) To determine whether there is sufficient evidence to charge him (s.37(1)). He must not delay charging to allow questioning to continue.

(c) If the suspect is not charged the custody officer may be required to release him. The presumption is that the suspect will be released with or without bail, but it can be rebutted if the custody officer has reasonable grounds for believing that detention without charge is necessary to secure or preserve evidence relating to the offence for which the suspect has been arrested, or to obtain such evidence by questioning him (s.37(2)).

(d) To keep the custody record which records the history of the detention (s.39(1)(b) and para.2 of the Code). The record is available to a solicitor or appropriate adult on arrival at the station and to the suspect on request for 12 months.

(e) To ensure that the suspect is treated in accordance with the provisions of the Act and the Code of Practice (see below).

(f) To itemise the suspect's property (see above).

(g) To inform the suspect of the reason for the detention, of his right to legal advice and his right to have a person informed that he is in custody and his right to consult the Codes of Practice. He should not, however, put specific questions to the suspect regarding his involvement in any offence, etc.

The right to legal advice and to have a person informed

A person who is in police detention is entitled to consult a solicitor privately at any time (s.58). The suspect must be told of this right both orally and in writing and will be asked to sign the custody record saying that this has been done. The availability of legal aid must be drawn to his attention and a poster outlining the right to legal advice must be displayed prominently in the charging area. The Code of Practice emphasises that no attempt should be made to dissuade a person from obtaining legal advice.

The suspect also has the right to have one person informed that he is in custody. That person may be a friend, a relative or other person who is likely to take an interest in his welfare (s.56, para.5 Code).

These are not absolute rights. In the case of serious arrestable offences the s.56 right can be postponed for up to 36 hours on the authority of an officer of at least the rank of inspector and in the case of s.58, a superintendent, if that officer has reasonable grounds for believing that the exercise of either right would:

(a) lead to interference with evidence connected with a serious arrestable offence;

(b) lead to interference with or physical injury to other persons;

(c) "tip-off" other persons suspected of a serious arrestable offence;

(d) hinder the recovery of property;

(e) hinder the recovery of proceeds from drug trafficking.

Delay may also be authorised under the Terrorism Act 2000.

It is not sufficient reason for postponement of these rights that a solicitor might advise his client to remain silent (*R. v Neil McIvor* (CC, 1987)). There must be a belief that the solicitor would commit the criminal offence of alerting other suspects or be hoodwinked into doing so inadvertently or unwittingly. In *R. v Samuel* (CA, 1988), the court felt that either belief could only rarely be genuinely held by the police and if substantiated, the suspect should be offered access to another solicitor.

Serious arrestable offences—definition—section 116

1. Some arrestable offences are so serious that they are always serious arrestable offences. These are listed in Sch.5 of the Act and include murder, manslaughter, rape, treason, kidnapping, causing explosions likely to endanger life or property and hijacking.
2. Any other arrestable offence may be serious if its commission has led to or is likely to lead to:
   (a) serious harm to the security of the state or public order;
   (b) serious interference with the administration of justice or with the investigation of offences;
   (c) death;
   (d) serious injury;
   (e) substantial financial gain or serious financial loss. (Loss is serious if it is serious for the person who suffers it.)

This last ground has given rise to some difficulty in interpretation. Clearly the intention was that run of the mill thefts should not be serious arrestable offences. In *R. v Neil McIvor* the court held that the police had wrongly considered the theft of 28 dogs owned by a hunt as a serious arrestable offence as the loss to the members of the hunt could not be considered a serious financial loss. In *R. v Eric Smith* (Crown Ct., 1987), it was felt that the police had wrongly considered a theft totalling £1,000 from a large company a serious arrestable offence. It would not be considered a serious loss by the company and the financial gain to the robbers was not necessarily substantial. However in *R. v Samuel* the theft of £300 from a building society was considered a serious arrestable offence, both because of the use of a sawn-off shot gun in the raid and also because of the accused's intention to cause serious financial loss to the building society.

The exercise of these rights

The Code says that consultation with a solicitor can be in person, in writing or by telephone. Note the use of the Duty Solicitor Scheme and the provision of free legal advice under the Green Form Scheme to facilitate this. About one third of suspects exercise this right. Much of this advice has been given by clerks rather than solicitors and the quality of the advice given has been questioned. In 1994 the Law Society and the Legal Aid Board initiated a training package "Police Station Skills for Legal Advisers" and an accreditation scheme, in an attempt to improve matters.

Even where there is an absolute right to legal advice, the suspect can be questioned before that advice is given if he consents, or where, to wait, would cause unreasonable delay or hindrance.

Solicitors may be present during the suspect's interview but the Code says that they may be asked to leave if their conduct prevents the investigating officer properly questioning the suspect. Such an exclusion might entail the solicitor being reported to the Law Society.

Where a relative or friend of a person in custody inquires as to his whereabouts, that person should normally be told unless the detainee objects or unless any of the factors, noted above, justifying delay, apply. The Code provides additional safeguards for juveniles, mentally handicapped persons, the deaf and those who cannot speak or understand English. (See, for example, paras 3.12 and 3.13 of Code C.)

The interview

It is the responsibility of the Custody Officer to ensure that detainees are treated in accordance with the Act and the Codes of Practice (s.39(1)).

Under para.12.1 of the Code, the Custody Officer has the power to decide whether the suspect can be interviewed by another officer. In the case of a dispute between the Custody Officer and investigating officer (who may often outrank him), s.39(6) provides that the matter should be referred to an officer of the rank of superintendent or above. The Code requires that there be an adequate record of the interview, that the suspect is given refreshments and allowed periods of rest during extended questioning. Para.12.2 provides that, in any 24 hour period, a suspect must normally be given eight hours rest. This should normally be at night. Questioning must not be oppressive. The purpose of any interview is not necessarily to obtain an admission but to obtain from the suspect his explanation of the facts.

As soon as the investigating officer believes that a prosecution should be brought and there is sufficient evidence for it to succeed, questioning should cease.

Review of detention

An important safeguard introduced by PACE is the periodic review of detention to see if such detention is justified in terms of the detention criteria in s.37(2) noted above. After initial consideration by the custody officer, the responsibility for the reviews rests with the *review officer* who, under s.40(1)(b), must be an officer of at least the rank of inspector and who has not been directly involved in the investigation. Where a person has been arrested and charged, the review officer is the Custody Officer. The first review takes place not later than six hours from the time the detention was authorised. The second review should not be later than nine hours after the first, *i.e.* 15 hours after the detention was authorised. Subsequent reviews should take place every nine hours thereafter. In *Roberts v Chief Constable of Cheshire* (HC, 1999), failure to carry out a timely review of detention, rendered the previously lawful detention, unlawful and entitled the suspect to claim damages. The obligation to review continues throughout the detention period.

Limits on period of detention without charge

The initial period of detention is 24 hours. Following the Criminal Justice Act 2003, s.7, the superintendent responsible for the station where the detainee is being held can extend this period for a further 12 hours. Further detention beyond the 36 hour point can only be authorised under a warrant of further detention issued by magistrates under s.43 if:

(a) it is a serious arrestable offence;
(b) the detention conditions apply;
(c) the investigation is being conducted diligently and expeditiously.

This authorises further detention for periods up to 36 hours. Further applications can be made for extensions up to a maximum of 96 hours from the commencement of the detention. At 96 hours, the suspect must be either charged or released.

The detention clock

In calculating the time limits for detention, the starting point is:

- (a) where a person has been arrested outside the police station—
  - (i) the time he arrives at the relevant station; or
  - (ii) the time 24 hours after the time of his arrest, whichever is the earlier;
- (b) where a person attends the police station voluntarily and is subsequently arrested there—the time of arrest.

There are special provisions where a person is arrested in another part of the country or abroad.

Applications to a magistrate should, if possible, be made during normal sittings and, in any event, not between 9pm and 10am. Section 43(5) gives a six-hour leeway at the 36 hour point in that an application for a warrant of further detention can be made up to 42 hours from the commencement of the detention clock, in a situation where the 36 hour period runs out at a time when it is not possible for a magistrate's court to sit. If, however, it was reasonable for the police to make the application in time, the magistrates must dismiss any application made after the 36 hour point. (See *R. v Slough JJ. Ex p. Stirling* (HC, 1987)).

The suspect or his solicitor is entitled to make representations to the reviewing officer as to why he should be released. A decision to continue the detention must be recorded in the suspect's custody record with reasons. Where an application for further detention is sought, the suspect must be taken before the magistrates and provided with a copy of the police information against him. He has a right to legal aid and legal representation.

Section 306 of the Criminal Justice Act 2003 extends the period for which those suspected of terrorist offences under s.41 of the Terrorist Act 2000 can be detained to 14 days without charge.

Detention after charge

Section 38(1) allows this:

(1) if necessary to substantiate a name or address;
(2) if the custody officer has reasonable grounds for believing this is necessary;
    (i) for the suspect's own protection;
    (ii) to prevent him from causing physical injury to any other person;
    (iii) to prevent loss or damage to property;
    (iv) to ensure his appearance in court;
(v) to prevent interference with the administration of justice or with the investigation of offences;
(vi) juveniles can also be detained in custody if the custody officer believes this to be in the juvenile's own interests.

Otherwise under s.46(2) the accused should be brought before a magistrate as soon as is practicable and in any event, not later than the first sitting after he has been charged. There are detailed provisions for the arranging of special sittings if no regular court is scheduled for the day the accused is charged or the following day.

POWERS OF ENTRY AND SEARCH

Police powers to enter premises come from the following sources:

1. Consent of the occupier.
2. Under statutory power.
3. By virtue of a warrant.

Premises are defined in s.23 of PACE and include any place and, in particular, any vehicle, vessel, aircraft, tent, etc.

Article 8(2) of the ECHR only permits a public authority to interfere with an individual's right to respect for his home etc, in accordance with the law and where necessary in a democratic society for the prevention of disorder or crime. To comply with this, any power of search must be clearly delineated and must be used proportionately. Thus Code of Practice B which applies to all searches, states that as the right to privacy and respect for personal property are key principles of the Human Rights Act, powers of entry, search and seizure should be clearly justified. Powers should be exercised courteously, with respect for persons and property. Reasonable force may be used only where necessary and must be proportionate to the circumstances.

Consent

It is estimated that the largest proportion of entries and searches takes place following the consent of the occupier. In the past it has been alleged that consent was often less than genuine, the person believing that he had no option but to allow the police the right to enter the premises and search. Code of Practice B recognises that consent must mean real consent. The occupier must be told that he can refuse to allow the search and that anything seized may be used in evidence. It provides that if consent is given, it must if practicable be in writing. The police must satisfy themselves that the person is in a position to give such consent.

Statutory powers of entry

(a) To execute a warrant of arrest (s.17(1)(a)). To arrest for an arrestable offence (s.17(1)(b)). To arrest for offences under the Public Order Act 1986 and the Criminal Law Act 1977 (s.17(1)(c)).

(b) To recapture a person who is unlawfully at large and whom the officer is hotly pursuing (s.17(1)(d)).

(c) To save life and limb or serious damage to property (s.17(1)(e)). The ambit of this appears very wide. While not a new power, it was one not greatly recognised or understood at common law.

(d) Although all other common law powers are abolished, s.17(6) retains the common law power of entry to deal with or prevent a breach of the peace (*Thomas v Sawkins* (HC, 1935)).

(e) There still exist other statutes which authorise the police and/or other officials to enter premises without a warrant, *e.g.* Customs and Excise Management Act 1979, s.84(5) which allows entry to a place where there are reasonable grounds to suspect signals or messages being sent to smugglers and various statutes giving powers of entry to Electricity and Trading Standards Officers and Firemen. The precise requirements, such as the need for written authority, vary from statute to statute.

(f) Special provisions permitting covert entry by police, customs etc. are contained in the Police Act 1997.

Statutory powers of search

(a) Following the arrest of a suspect for an arrestable offence, there is a power under s.18 to search the suspect's premises for evidence relating to the offence, or some connected or similar arrestable offence. If necessary, a police officer can search under this section before taking the suspect to the police station (s.18(5)). Apart from this, such a search must be authorised by an officer of the rank of inspector or above. The phrase "similar" is likely to lead to difficulty.

(b) Section 32(2)(b), dealing with the search of anyone arrested for any offence, arrestable or otherwise, allows the police to enter and search the premises where the suspect was at the time of his arrest or immediately before for evidence relating to the offence for which he was arrested. The search must be no more than reasonably required for the purposes of discovering such evidence and there must be reasonable grounds for believing that such evidence will be found. This is an immediate power which must be exercised at the time of the arrest *R. v Badham* (1987)).

Search warrants

There are a number of Acts of Parliament which empower a magistrate on sworn information to issue a warrant to search for such things as stolen goods, forged documents, drugs and evidence of a serious arrestable offence. If it is thought that the search might have an adverse effect on good community relations, the officer in charge should normally consult the local police community relations officer before proceeding with the application. The warrant should identify the legal authority for the application, the premises to be searched, the object of the search and the grounds for undertaking the search.

Items subject to legal privilege

This broadly relates to communications between lawyer and client either in relation to the giving of legal advice or in contemplation of legal proceedings. In *R. v Snaresbrook Crown Court Ex p.* DPP (DC, 1988), a legal aid application was held to be subject to legal privilege. Items held with the intention of furthering a criminal purpose are excluded from this category (see *R. v Central Criminal Court Ex p. Francis and Francis* (HC, 1988)). No warrant can be obtained to seize such material. Even if the police "chance" upon it in the course of a legal search, it cannot be taken.

Excluded material

As defined in s.11, this includes journalistic material held in confidence and confidential personal records held by such people as doctors, social workers, etc. No new rights to such material are given by the Act but it does standardise the procedure for applying for a warrant to obtain such material. Applications must be made to a circuit judge. In *R. v Central Criminal Court Ex p. Brown* (DC, 1992), it was held that a judge had no power to issue a warrant to obtain hospital records under s.9 as there had been no right to obtain the materials before PACE.

Special procedure material

Consists of other types of confidential material which does not fall within the definition of excluded material in s.11. It includes material held in confidence which is not classed as "personal records" and certain types of journalistic material not caught by the definition in s.13. Access to special procedure material can only be obtained by virtue of a warrant issued by a circuit judge. For examples see *R. v Bristol Crown Court Ex p. Bristol Press and Picture Agency Ltd* (HC, 1987) and *Re An Application under s.9 of the Police and Criminal Evidence Act 1984* (HC, 1988).

The conduct of the search

Code B emphasises:

(a) Searches must be made at a reasonable hour unless this might frustrate the purpose of the search (para.5.2).
(b) Unless impossible or would, for example, frustrate the search by losing the element of surprise, the police should attempt to explain to the occupant the authority for the search and obtain consent. In *O'Loughlin v Chief Constable of Essex* (CA, 1988), failure to do this meant that the police were trespassers.

(c) Where such consent is refused or the premises are unoc-
cupied, reasonable force may be used to effect entry. In
Murgatroyd v CC of West Yorkshire (CA, 2000), the use of a
police dog in forcing an entry under s.17(1)(e) was considered an unreasonable use of force.

(d) Any occupier should be served, where practicable, with a
standard notice of powers and rights. This explains the
basis on which the search was made and explains the
rights of the occupier.

(e) Premises may not be ransacked but searched only to the
extent necessary to achieve the objects of the search.

(f) Searches must be conducted with due consideration.

(g) The search should be discontinued if it becomes clear that
the items sought are not on the premises.

The extent of the search and seizure

Where the police are searching by virtue of a warrant, s.16(8)
states that the search may only be to the extent required for the
purpose for which the warrant was issued. Where entry is
justified under s.17, the power to search is only to the extent
reasonably required for the purpose for which the power of
entry was exercised.

Section 18 allows the police to search for evidence relating to
the offence for which the suspect has been arrested or evidence
relating to some other arrestable offence which is connected
with or similar to that offence. The s.32 power is narrower in
that it only permits premises to be searched for evidence
relating to the offence for which the suspect has been arrested.

In all instances there is an accompanying power of seizure. In
addition where the police chance upon evidence for which they
had no power to search, the common law gave further powers
of seizure. In *Ghani v Jones* (CA, 1970) additional powers of
seizure would be given if there were reasonable grounds for
believing that a serious crime had been committed, so serious
that it was of first importance that offenders be brought to
justice, that the item seized was the fruit of crime or material
evidence to prove the commission of the crime, that it was
unreasonable for the person in possession of the evidence to
refuse to hand it over and that it was not kept any longer than
necessary by the police. PACE, s.19 may also give a power of
seizure. If the police are lawfully on the premises they may seize
other evidence if they have reasonable grounds to believe either

that it has been obtained in consequence of the commission of an offence or that it is evidence in relation to an offence which he is investigating or any other offence. In either case the officer must have reasonable grounds for believing that it is necessary to seize the evidence there and then to prevent it being destroyed.

In *Cowan v The Commissioner of Police for the Metropolis* (CA, 1999) it was held that s.19 covered seizure of a vehicle. A vehicle falls within the definition of "premises" and where the nature of the premises made it physically possible for these to be seized and where practical considerations made this desirable, such a seizure was permissible.

The Criminal Justice and Police Act 2001 allows the police to remove items for sifting and examination elsewhere when it is not practical to do this on the spot.

Effect of non-compliance with PACE

Evidence obtained in breach of PACE and the Codes may be excluded by virtue of ss.76 and 78. A distinction is drawn between confession and other evidence.

Section 76 confessions

If it is alleged that a confession has been obtained by oppression or in consequence of anything likely to render it unreliable, the court will not admit it unless the prosecution can prove beyond reasonable doubt that it was not obtained in this way. Oppression may include torture, degrading treatment or the use or threat of violence. It may also arise from "the exercise of authority in a burdensome, harsh or wrongful manner; unjust or cruel treatment." (See *Fulling* (CA, 1987)).

Bullying or hectoring by police officers might also constitute oppression (*Paris* (CA, 1982)).

In determining whether anything said or done was likely to render a confession unreliable, the character of the accused will be relevant. So, for example, failure to allow access to a solicitor may constitute oppression in the case of an accused of low intelligence but may not if he is an experienced offender. (See *Alladice* (CA, 1988) and *Weeks* (CA, 1994).)

Section 78

The court has a discretion to exclude any evidence, including confessions if it appears to the court, having regard to all the circumstances, that its admission would have such an adverse effect on the fairness of the proceedings that the court ought not to admit it. Failure to comply with provisions of PACE and the accompanying Codes of Practice might be considered to have such an effect. This will be particularly likely if there has been a series of breaches. In *Canale* (CA, 1990) the court exercised its discretion to exclude evidence where the breaches were seen to be "flagrant, deliberate and cynical". In *Keenan* (CA, 1990) the court said that, to persuade the court to exercise its discretion to exclude evidence, the breaches must be "significant and substantial." Such breaches as denial of access to a solicitor (*Samuel* (1988)) and failure to tell a suspect of his right to legal advice (*Absolam* (CA, 1989)) have been viewed as particularly serious. Evidence has also been excluded as a result of failing to keep a proper record of the interview (*Walsh* (CA, 1989)) and a series of breaches of the Code which, whilst individually were minor, cumulatively were sufficient to cast doubt on the fairness of the proceedings (*Canale*, above).

The use of such evidence may also be subject to challenge as a breach of Art.6 ECHR in that its admission interferes with the right to a fair trial.

POLICE MISCONDUCT

Remedies for unlawful arrest and detention

A basic principle of the rule of law is that any interference with the liberty of the individual must be justified by law. Simply by virtue of his official position no police officer has the right to interfere with a person's liberty unless he can point to legal authority to justify his actions. If a person is detained irregularly or his property or person searched without lawful authority, he has the following remedies:

1. Self Defence. If a person is unlawfully restrained he is entitled to use reasonable force to effect his escape (*Kenlin v Gardner* (HC, 1967)). This remedy must be pursued with caution as the amount of force used must be no more than is reasonable in the circumstances. If excessive it may constitute an assault (*Fagan v MPC* (HC, 1968)). This may be a very nice judgment to make in a stressful situation.
2. An action of damages may be brought for false imprisonment, wrongful arrest, etc.

3. An application for a writ of *habeas corpus*. The system of review of detention introduced under PACE does not affect the system of applications for *habeas corpus*. An ex parte application is made, supported by an affidavit.
4. Action of damages for trespass to the person, or trespass to goods.
5. A person whose chattels have been seized by the police can apply for an order for delivery of the goods and damages under s.3 of the Torts (Interference with Goods) Act 1977.
6. Complaint against the police.

It should be noted that breach of the Codes of Practice does not, of itself, render the police officer liable to any criminal or civil proceedings. The court can, however, take such a breach into account where relevant.

Complaints against the police

It was felt by the Royal Commission on Police Powers that criminal prosecution and investigation could only work well if the general public felt confident in the role played by the police. Before 1976 investigation of complaints was essentially an internal police matter. In 1976 the Police Complaints Board was established with limited functions to oversee the disciplining of police officers, who had contravened the Police Disciplinary Code but had not faced criminal charges. It had no powers in relation to criminal actions against the police and no powers of investigation. In 1984 it became known as the Police Complaints Authority with greater supervisory powers. Nevertheless public confidence in the system remained low particularly among members of minority ethnic communities. A number of well publicised cases have illustrated the difficulties facing investigations of complaints where there are no independent witnesses. A further concern related to the number of complaints withdrawn before investigation leading to fears that undue pressure was being brought to bear on complainants.

The reluctance of the DPP to prosecute police officers has also attracted criticism. He operates on the basis that there must be a reasonable prospect that a jury is more likely to convict than acquit on the evidence, the 51 per cent rule. The DPP has said that experience has shown that stronger evidence is required than is the norm.

A new system for dealing with complaints was established under the Police Reform Act 2002 which set up the Independent Police Complaints Commission. This came into operation in April 2004. It has the power to conduct investigations itself or manage or supervise police investigations. It also has a wider responsibility to monitor and work to improve the way in which all complaints are handled by local police forces. The Chair is appointed by the Crown and the members by the Home Secretary.

Complaints may be brought by anyone who feels he is the victim of misconduct, anyone witnessing misconduct or any friend or representative of the victim. The system covers all ranks but does not deal with complaints about general policing policy.

The method of dealing with the complaint will depend on its nature. The majority of complaints are relatively minor and relate to such things as incivility. These are handled locally through a system of informal resolution, subject to the consent of the complainant. Complaints that require a formal investigation will either be investigated by the police or, in more serious cases , by the IPCC itself (Sch.3). The IPCC can supervise police investigations in certain circumstances and there is a right of appeal to it if the complainant is dissatisfied with the findings or the proposed outcomes of the investigation.

The decision whether to initiate criminal proceedings is taken by the DPP to whom allegations of criminal conduct must be reported.

---

5. PROTEST AND PUBLIC ORDER

The right to demonstrate against unpopular causes has long been considered a bulwark of liberty in any civilised society, enabling groups within that society to attempt to influence public opinion, to express their solidarity, to pressurise government and publicise their cause. Accordingly, the constitutions of many states contain guarantees of the right of peaceful protest.

In the United Kingdom there was no such positive statement of this or any other right. The approach taken was that any interference with individual liberty must be justified in terms of common law or statute (*Entick v Carrington* (1765)). An assembly or procession was not unlawful *per se,* unless, for example, it caused an obstruction or constituted a public nuisance. Prior permission was not required for a demonstration unless it was being held on private land or in some special location regulated by specific byelaws such as Trafalgar Square or the Royal Parks. As will be seen, the Public Order Act 1984 and the Criminal Justice and Public Order Act 1994 introduced additional controls such as the requirement to give notice of processions.

There was no obligation on the police to facilitate peaceful protest. Their fundamental duty was to preserve public order and they had wide ranging powers at their disposal to achieve this. Thus the law, rather than facilitating the right of peaceful protest, simply accepted that demonstrators could do what they liked providing they did not break the law, something it was very easy to do.

One basic restriction stemmed from the fact that the public was entitled to use the highway only for passage and repassage from one place to another and for matters incidental to that. In *Harrison v Duke of Rutland* (HC, 1893) it was held that a person who used the highway other than for passage could be sued for trespass. What constituted an approved incidental use appeared to be construed very narrowly. Improper use of the highway might also constitute a nuisance leading to criminal charges, a civil action of damages or an injunction prohibiting the con- tinuation of the improper use. For example, a demonstration outside a firm of estate agents was prohibited, although peaceful (*Hubbard v Pitt* (HC, 1976)).

In practice most demonstrations went ahead providing they were peaceful, well-organised and there was no actual obstruction.

The HRA changed the approach to protest and public order significantly by imposing a positive duty on the police, as a public authority, to promote convention rights.

Article 11 of the ECHR

Article 11 of the ECHR says that everyone has the right of peaceful assembly and to freedom of association with others. No restriction shall be placed on the exercise of these rights other than such as are prescribed by law and are necessary in a democratic society in the interests of national security or public safety, for the prevention of disorder or crime, for the protection of health or morals or the protection of the rights and freedoms of others.

In addition Art.10 ECHR provides that everyone has the right to freedom of expression. (Again subject to the same qualifications.)

Thus the right to demonstrate peacefully has now been recognised in positive terms. Any restrictions on the exercise of this right must be justified in terms of the qualifications. They must be proportionate. The police, as a public authority, must now act in a positive manner to uphold convention rights.

This change of approach was anticipated in *DPP v Jones* (HL, 1999). Jones had been convicted of trespassory assembly following a peaceful protest on the highway near Stonehenge. The House of Lords by a majority allowed the appeal, stating that a peaceful assembly on the highway did not necessarily exceed the public's right of access. Lord Irvine went further than the other judges in recognising a right of peaceful assembly on the highway saying that, otherwise, English law would be in direct conflict with the Convention.

The location of meetings and demonstrations

Any meeting on private premises must have the consent of the owner. The European Court of Human Rights held in *Appleby v UK* (2003) that there had been no violation of Art.10 where the owners of a shopping mall refused to allow demonstrators to campaign on their premises against a proposed development. In the past the law has largely dealt with trespassers by way of civil action. The Criminal Justice and Public Order Act 1994 indicated a clear movement towards criminal remedies. See for example the power to remove trespassers under s.61 which strengthens earlier powers and s.68 which is designed to deal with disruptive trespassers, who interfere with lawful activities through disruptive, obstructive or intimidating behaviour by the creation of the offence of "aggravated trespass".

By s.11 of the Public Order Act 1986, anyone organising a march must give the police six days notice otherwise he may commit an offence. When a march is organised at short notice, as much notice as is practicable must be given. The provision is designed to ensure that the policing of the demonstration can be properly planned.

THE POWERS OF THE POLICE

Statutory powers

The Public Order Act 1986 distinguishes between public processions and public assemblies. Public processions are defined in *Flockhart v Robinson* (HC 1950) as a body of persons moving along a route. A public assembly is defined in s.16 as an assembly of 20 or more persons in a public place that is wholly or partly open to the air.

Conditions

Section 12 of the Act gives the police the power to impose conditions on processions where there is a risk of serious public disorder, to prevent serious damage to property, serious disruption to the life of the community and to prevent intimidation. Such conditions may relate to route, size, timing, etc. of the march. Organising or participating in a march in breach of any such conditions constitutes an offence.

Under s.14 the police are given a parallel power to impose conditions on public assemblies. It would seem, in the light of the Human Rights Act that any such conditions must be proportionate.

The power to ban

If the s.12 powers are judged insufficient and there remains a risk of serious public disorder, there is a power, under s.13, to ban processions for any period up to three months. The Chief Officer of Police may apply to the local authority for a banning order which must be confirmed by the Home Secretary. It is an offence to organise, to participate in or to incite someone to participate in a banned march.

The ban is a blanket ban covering all marches or all marches of a particular class such as political marches. This has caused some concern as peaceful demonstrators may be prevented from marching because of the threat posed by a potentially disruptive counter-demonstration. Yet the suggestion that there should be a power to impose selective bans was rejected, neither police nor judges appearing willing to become involved in such a politically sensitive task, the exercise of which would certainly bring forth accusations of bias.

Section 70 of the 1994 Act introduced a power to ban trespassory assemblies for up to four days. These are defined as assemblies which involve at least 20 people, are held on land to which the public has limited or no rights of access and takes place without the permission of the occupier of the land.

Application must be made to the local authority by the chief officer of police on the basis that he believes that an assembly is intended to be held which might result in serious disruption to the life of the community or significant damage to land, building or monuments of historical, architectural or scientific importance. Such a ban may cover an area of not more than a five-mile radius.

Other statutory powers

Section 71 of the 1994 Act gives the police a power to prevent persons proceeding to banned trespassory assemblies. Note also the s.60 power to stop and search in anticipation of violence detailed in Ch.4 above.

The courts may have to consider whether the exercise of these various statutory rights is incompatible with protestors' convention rights, which the courts, as a public authority are under a positive duty to uphold.

Breach of the peace

At common law, the police have the power to take whatever action is necessary during a demonstration to prevent a breach of the peace. There have been conflicting views over the years as to what constitutes a breach of the peace.

It has been defined as something more than a mere disturbance of the public calm or quiet. An element of violence was deemed essential in *R. v Howell* (CA, 1982), and in *Percy v DPP* (DC, 1994) where the court, in determining whether the appellant should have been bound over to keep the peace, said that the test was whether there was a real risk of violence or threatened violence occurring. (Contrast this with *R. v The Chief Constable of Devon & Cornwall Ex p. CEGB* (CA, 1981) where Denning M.R. said that there would be a breach of the peace whenever a person, lawfully carrying out his work, is unlawfully and physically prevented by another from doing it.)

The violence need not always stem from the demonstrators. In *Nicol and Selvanayagam v DPP* (HC, 1995), demonstrators attempting to disrupt an angling competition by throwing twigs into the water were arrested and subsequently bound over to keep the peace although no violence or threats of violence against the anglers took place. It was sufficient that their conduct was unreasonable and interfered with a lawful activity. A natural consequence of the conduct would be to provoke violence in others. On the other hand in *Redmond-Bate v DPP* (CA, 1999) the court held that the police had acted unlawfully in arresting a speaker on the steps of Wakefield Cathedral who was drawing a hostile crowd. It was felt that her conduct was not unreasonable. See also *Steel and Others v UK* (ECHR, 1999). These cases do little to clarify the situation where it is clear that peaceful conduct is going to result in violent conduct by others. When does it become unreasonable for the peaceful protester to refuse to stop their protest and co-operate with the police?

This power has been used by the police in a variety of ways; to ask demonstrators to leave the scene, even when acting peacefully (*Duncan v Jones* (HC, 1936)); to justify the removal of provocative emblems or banners (*Humphries v Connor* (IR, 1864)); to direct a procession en route if a breach of the peace is reasonably apprehended (Lord Scarman's Report on the Red Lion Square Disorders). One of the most controversial uses of the power is to prevent demonstrators reaching the scene of the demonstration, a use upheld by the courts in *Moss & Others v McLachlan* (HC, 1984). The court held that, providing the police honestly and reasonably believed there was a real risk of a breach of the peace, they were entitled to take reasonable preventative action. What that action consisted of must depend on the imminence or immediacy of the threat to the peace. In *McConnell v Chief Constable of the Greater Manchester Police* (CA, 1990), the Court of Appeal confirmed that a breach of the peace could take place on private premises. If a meeting is held in private premises it should be noted that the police can insist on entering the premises even against the wishes of the organisers, if they have reasonable grounds to believe a breach of the peace is likely to occur (*Thomas v Sawkins* (HC, 1935)), a power confirmed in *McLeod v MPC* (CA, 1994).

Any such actions to prevent a breach of the peace must now be considered in the light of the Human Rights Act, the positive duty on the police to facilitate peaceful protest and the need to act proportionately. In *Laporte v The Chief Constable of Gloucestershire* (Admin C, 2004), the police detained a coach load of demonstrators en route to an anti-war rally at an RAF base and forced the coach to drive back to London without stopping. It was held that while the police were justified in preventing the demonstrators traveling to the air-base, their actions in escorting the coach back to London went much further than was necessary to prevent a breach of the peace.

PUBLIC ORDER OFFENCES

The major public order offences were put on a statutory basis by the Public Order Act 1986:

Riot (section 1)

This is the most serious of the offences in the Act, and is triable only on indictment and attracts a maximum penalty of ten years' imprisonment.

> "Where 12 or more persons who are present together use or threaten unlawful violence for a common purpose and the conduct of them (taken together) is such as would cause a person of reasonable firmness present at the scene to fear for his personal safety, each of the persons using unlawful violence for the common purpose is guilty of riot."

In order to obtain a conviction, it must be shown that the accused intends to use violence or is aware that his conduct may be violent.

It should be noted that while 12 persons must be present who are using or threatening violence, only the person charged need be shown to have intended to use the violence. The offence can be committed by aiders and abettors as well as by principals (R. *v Jefferson* (CA, 1994)). It is unclear the extent to which the 12 need form a cohesive group. Section 8 says that violence means any violent conduct towards persons or property. It is unnecessary to produce a person who fears for his safety. The test is whether a hypothetical bystander of the requisite firmness would suffer such fear.

Violent disorder (section 2)

This is the normal charge for serious outbreaks of public disorder.

> "Where three or more persons who are present together, use or threaten unlawful violence and the conduct of them (taken

together) is such as would cause a person of reasonable firmness present at the scene to fear for his personal safety, each of the persons using or threatening violence is guilty of violent disorder."

It should be noted that the persons present need not have a common purpose (*R. v Mahroof* (CA, 1988)) but that all three must be using or threatening violence (*R. v McGuigan & Cameron* (CA, 1991)); that once again it is unnecessary to produce a frightened bystander; and that unlike riot, it is sufficient to intend to threaten violence.

Affray (section 3)

This is intended to penalise fighting in that "a person is guilty of affray if he uses or threatens violence towards another and his conduct is such as would cause a person of reasonable firmness present at the scene to fear for his personal safety."

Again no frightened bystander need be present. The standard is whether a hypothetical bystander of reasonable firmness would fear for his safety. (See *R. v Davison* (CA, 1992).) As with ss.1–2, the offence need not be committed in a public place. However, unlike the other offences under the Act, the violence must be directed against the person and must be more than mere threatening words. In *R. v Dixon* (DC, 1993), the accused ordered his Alsatian to "kill the officer". He appealed against conviction claiming that he had merely used words. The court, while accepting that the offence could not be committed by words alone, dismissed the appeal on the ground that the dog had been used as a weapon.

Threatening, abusive and insulting behaviour (section 4)

This replaced s.5 of the Public Order Act 1936 which had long been the main public order offence and which had been used in a wide range of situations including demonstrations, football hooliganism, "streaking" and industrial disputes.

"A person is guilty of an offence if he
(a) uses towards another person threatening, abusive or insulting words or behaviour, or
(b) distributes or displays to another person any writing, sign . . . which is threatening, abusive or insulting . . . with intent to cause another to believe that immediate violence will be used . . . or to provoke (such) violence."

The consequences feared or provoked must be immediate, unlawful violence not violence at some unspecified future time.

(*R. v Horseferry Road Stipendiary Magistrate Ex p. Siadatan* (DC 1991).)

The phrase "threatening, abusive or insulting" is likely to be interpreted as under the Public Order Act 1936. In *Brutus v Cozens* (HL, 1973) Lord Reid said that the words must be given their ordinary English meaning. They must be more than vigorous or unmannerly. The audience must feel threatened, abused or insulted.

Under s.6(3) a person is guilty of an offence under s.4 only if he intends his words, behaviour or writing, etc. to be threatening, abusive or insulting or is aware that it may be threatening, abusive or insulting. (*DPP v Clarke* (DC, 1991).) The offence can be committed in public or private, but the Act is drafted in such a way as to exclude domestic disputes (s.4(2)). (See *Atkin v DPP* (DC, 1989).) It should be noted that in this offence we are not dealing with the hypothetical bystander. The conduct must be directed to another person and it is the reactions of that other person which matter. The speaker must take his audience as he finds it (*Jordan v Burgoyne* (HC, 1963)).

Intentionally causing harassment alarm or distress (section 4A)

Section 154 of the 1994 Act created a new offence which was designed primarily to deal with cases of serious racial harassment although not confined to use in this context. It makes it an offence to intentionally cause harassment, alarm or distress by using threatening, abusive or insulting words or behaviour. It is seen as more serious than the s.5 offence and attracts a maximum penalty of six months' imprisonment or a level 5 fine or both.

Offensive conduct (section 5)

This is used for minor acts of disorder such as shouting and swearing which are likely to cause alarm or distress, displaying abusive or insulting slogans or throwing over dustbins and banging on doors in the common parts of blocks of flats. It would cover those minor disturbances formerly dealt with under s.5 of the Public Order Act 1936 but also types of anti-social behaviour which have not been criminalised in the past.

"A person is guilty of an offence if he

   (a) uses threatening, abusive or insulting words or behaviour, or disorderly behaviour, or

   (b) displays any writing sign or visible representation which is threatening, abusive or insulting, within the hearing or sight of a person likely to be caused harassment alarm or distress thereby."

In *DPP v Clarke, Lewis, O'Connell & O'Keefe* (DC, 1992) it was held that, for a conviction, the accused must intend their behaviour to be threatening, etc. or be aware that it might be. It is not, however, necessary to prove actual harm or distress.

Section 5(4) gives the police the power of summary arrest for this offence if the person persists in the conduct after being warned to stop. (See *Groom v DPP* (HC, 1991).)

The imprecision of this offence has caused concern in that it leaves the police considerable discretion as to what type of conduct is unacceptable and, indeed, a recent research study has shown wide variation in its use from one police force to another. In the context of a demonstration or industrial dispute, participants may well shout slogans which are abusive and are likely to cause distress to those who disagreed with the cause in question. The Law Commission proposing the offence had confined it to situations where the alarm or distress experienced was "substantial" but this requirement was dropped from the Act itself. The court in *DPP v Orum* (DC, 1989) accepted that in appropriate circumstances police officers could be caused the necessary "harassment, alarm or distress." The use of the section has been wide-ranging. In *Vignon v DPP* (DC, 1997) for example, it was used against a market stall holder who installed a camera to spy on customers in the changing room. In fact the greatest single use of the section relates to insults directed at the police.

Using s.5 to restrict protest may infringe rights under Art.10(2) of the Convention. In *Percy v DPP* (2002), a conviction under s.5, which resulted from a demonstrator defacing a US flag during a demonstration against US foreign policy, was quashed as being in in breach of Art.10. Contrast this, however, with *Harry John Hammond v DPP* (DC, 2004) where H, an evangelical Christian preaching in public and displaying signs condemning homosexuality and lesbianism, was convicted under s.5. His appeal on the ground that this was an unjustifiable restriction of his freedom of expression under Art.10 was rejected as the restriction was required in order to show tolerance to others.

The Crime and Disorder Act 1998 creates several more serious offences based on ss.4 and 5 where the conduct is racially aggravated.

Other public order offences

Sections 1 and 2 of the 1936 Act make:

(i) the wearing of a uniform signifying association with a political organisation or with the promotion of any political objective, an offence. For the rather wide definition of "uniform" see *O'Moran v DPP* (HC, 1975);
(ii) the organisation or training of a body whose purpose is either;
    (a) to usurp the function of the police or the armed forces; or
    (b) to use or display force in an attempt to achieve a political objective, an offence.

The Public Order Act 1986 does not codify the law and must be seen against a background of common law. There remain a number of other offences which can be used in a public order situation. These include obstructing the police in the execution of their duty (see s.89(2) Police Act 1996 and *Duncan v Jones* (1936)); obstructing the Highway under s.137 of the Highways Act 1980; note also the use of binding over orders.

RESPONSIBILITY FOR THE POLICE

There is no national police force in Britain. Instead there are local forces historically based on the counties with various amalgamations. In London there is the Metropolitan Police. Although separate and independent, they share an increasing number of centralised resources such as the police national computer and the national reporting centre. There is a national pay structure and terms and conditions of employment. It is felt that the increased provision of services on a national basis will lead to increased centralisation. The Police Act 1997 continued the trend with the establishment of a National Criminal Intelligence Service Authority, a National Crime Squad and a Police Information Technology Organisation.

Under the Police Act 1964 control of the police was shared between the Home Secretary, the Police Authority and the Chief

Constable (Metropolitan Police Commissioner in London). This division of authority was referred to as a system of "tripartite control".

The Home Secretary had a general duty under the 1964 Act to promote the efficiency of the police. In fact he had considerable power and influence which arose from his financial controls, his control over the appointment and dismissal of chief constables, control over training and equipment and his ability to regulate standards through the inspection system. In addition, extensive guidance was given by Home Office Circular.

Police Authorities were Local Authority Committees made up of 2/3 councillors and 1/3 magistrates. They had a statutory responsibility to maintain "an adequate and efficient police force for the area". This rather vague phrase had traditionally led them to concentrate on buildings and equipment although, during the 1980s, some police authorities tried to influence styles of policing, for example, by refusing to pay for certain types of riot control equipment. The decision in *R. v Secretary of State for the Home Department Ex p. Northumbria Police Authority* (HL, 1988), which confirmed the Home Secretary's power to provide such equipment if he so wished, severely limited this tactic as a method of control.

The Chief Constable had operational control and was subject to no-one for the way in which he deployed his resources.

The reforms

The 1994 Reforms, now consolidated in the Police Act 1996 as amended by the Police Reform Act 2002, were said by the Government to be driven by the need to give the Home Secretary more direct control over the strategy and framework for policing and to give Police Authorities more opportunity to take key decisions locally, setting their own budgets and determining local strategies for policing. Critics responded that the changes would increase centralised control of the police. It was alleged that the increased powers given to Police Authorities were illusory, that it was "responsibility without power".

The role of the Home Secretary

Section 36 of the 1996 Act and the Police Reform Act 2002 impose a duty on the Home Secretary to exercise his powers in a manner and to such an extent as appears to him to be calculated to promote the efficiency and effectiveness of the police. His specific powers include:

(a) the setting of national priorities and a national policing plan—s.1 of 2002 Act;
(b) the setting of objectives for Police Authorities—s.37;
(c) the issuing of Codes of practice for chief officers to promote efficiency and effectiveness;
(d) the setting of performance targets for the achievement of these—s.38;
(e) the power to give directions to police authorities following adverse inspection reports—s.40 and s.4 of 2002 Act;
(f) the power to require special reports ss.43 and 44 and cause local inquiries to be held—s.49, and powers further strengthened by s.3 of 2002 Act;
(g) wide powers to make regulations re discipline, training, equipment, the government, administration and conditions of service—s.50;
(h) control over appointment and dismissal of Chief Constables and Deputies. (In 2004 the Home Secretary initiated procedures for the removal of the Chief Constable of Humberside following criticism of his force in the investigation which followed the Soham murders in the interest of efficiency and effectiveness and to maintain public confidence. This power was confirmed by the High Court.)
(i) financial controls; and
(j) inspection through Her Majesty's Inspectors of Constabulary.

The cumulative effect of these has been to increase the effective controls available to the Home Secretary.

Police authorities

For every police area there is a police authority. In most cases it is made up of nine councillors, three magistrates and five independent members. The independent members are appointed by the police authority from a list of suitable candidates. These are recruited by advert and then interviewed and selected by a panel representing the police authority, the Home Secretary and a third member chosen by the other two. This complicated procedure was introduced to alleviate fears that the

Home Secretary would have too great an influence over police authorities.

The function of the police authority is outlined in s.6 of the Act which states that it shall be the duty of the police authority to secure the maintenance of an efficient and effective police force for the area. In doing this it has to have regard for those national objectives set by the Home Secretary and its own local objectives, performance targets and local policing plan. This plan, the draft of which will have been produced by the Chief Constable following local consultation, will include a statement of policing priorities and the authority's financial allocations. An important function of the police authority is to monitor the force's performance against this plan and produce an Annual Report.

The Chief Constable

In the Metropolitan area of London, the Chief officer of Police is the Metropolitan Police Commissioner. Otherwise, under s.10 each police force is under the direction and control of the Chief Constable and, as will be seen, the courts are extremely unwilling to interfere with the way he settles general policies and concentrates resources. It has been argued that the effect of the 1996 Act has been to restrict the freedom of the Chief Constable in that he has to produce a local policing plan which takes into account both national and local objectives and sets performance targets. Inevitably this must affect decisions on allocation of resources.

The courts

There are many illustrations of the courts' reluctance to interfere with the Chief Constable's operational decisions. In *R. v Metropolitan Police Commissioner Ex p. Blackburn* (CA, 1968), Lord Denning said that while chief officers of police are answerable to law, there are many fields in which they have a discretion with which the law will not interfere. "It is for the Chief Constable . . . to decide in any particular case whether enquiries should be pursued or whether an arrest should be made . . . It must be for him to decide on the disposition of his force and the concentration of his resources on any particular crime or area." In *R. v Chief Constable of Devon and Cornwall Ex p. CEGB* (CA, 1981) the court refused to issue a mandamus ordering the Chief Constable to assist the CEGB in clearing a site of demonstrators who were impeding survey work for a new nuclear power station as it could not tell the Chief Constable how he should respond to the situation as it could not judge the explosiveness of the situation at the time. In *R. v Chief Constable of Sussex Ex p. International Traders Ferry Ltd* (CA, 1997), the court said that it would only interfere if the decision was irrational, so manifestly unreasonable that the court could interfere on "Wednesbury" grounds. (See Ch.6.)

The courts have also refused to interfere with a policy direction not to enforce a particular law. In *R. v Metropolitan Police Commissioner Ex p. Blackburn No.3* (CA, 1973) it was alleged that the Metropolitan Police Commissioner had issued an illegal policy directive in ordering his men not to enforce the provisions of the Obscene Publications Act 1959. The court refused to issue an order of mandamus on the ground that it had not been established that such a blanket directive had been issued and that it was within his rights to deploy his forces as he wished.

Quite clearly, however, he does not have unlimited discretion. He has a duty to enforce the law of the land. So, for example, the courts have indicated that they would interfere if a Chief Constable decided not to take action against housebreakers in any circumstances. (See also *R. v Oxford Ex p. Levey* (HC, 1987).)

6. JUDICIAL REVIEW

If an individual has suffered a grievance at the hands of a public body, he may be able to obtain redress through the courts. In addition to any statutory rights of appeal, there may be a right to invoke the inherent supervisory jurisdiction of the High Court. This enables the Court to review the decisions of government ministers, inferior courts, tribunals and other administrative bodies to ensure that they do not act illegally, irrationally or commit some procedural impropriety (*per* Lord Diplock in *CCSU v The Minister for the Civil Service* (HL, 1984)). It must be stressed that the courts are not challenging the merits of the decision but rather whether it is a decision the body is entitled to make, a point emphasised by Lord Scarman in *Not-*

tinghamshire CC v Secretary of State for the Environment (HL, 1986), when he said "Judicial review is a great weapon in the hands of the judges; but the judges must observe the constitutional limits set by our parliamentary system on their exercise of this beneficient power."

Historically, the basis of the court's intervention was the *ultra vires* doctrine. If a body exercising statutory powers went beyond the four corners of the Act, then the court could intervene. This might occur in a number of ways. For example, the body might be exercising the wrong powers or may be taking the wrong type of decision. In *Att-Gen v Fulham Corporation* (HC, 1921) the Local Authority had power under the Baths and Wash Houses Acts 1846–1878 to establish baths, wash houses and open bathing places. The court held that this did not give it the power to operate a commercial laundry. The court must consider what is the area over which power is given. Any exercise of power by the authority which falls outside that area will be *ultra vires.*

Then again a statute might prescribe that the power should be exercised by a named person or a person with specific qualifications. If the power is exercised by another it may be an *ultra vires* act which is a nullity. In *Anisminic v Foreign Compensation Commission* (CA, 1968), Lord Diplock described such misuse of power as *excess of jurisdiction.*

The doctrine of *ultra vires* was used not simply to control the scope of the power being exercised but also to control the way it was used. So where a body used its power in a manifestly unreasonable manner, acted in bad faith, refused to take relevant factors into account in reaching its decision or based its decision on irrelevant ones, the court would intervene on the ground that the body had abused its power. (See Lord Reid in *Anisminic* (HL, 1969).) The basis of the control was that the courts considered that when Parliament gave a body statutory power to act, it could be implied that Parliament intended it to act in a particular way; in good faith, in a reasonable manner, in accordance with the requirements of natural justice. It must be said, however, that in attempting to control such abuse of power, the courts blurred the distinction between the merits of the decision and its *vires.* This could be seen particularly in cases such as *Congrieve v The Home Office* (CA, 1976).

In recent years the courts have extended their supervisory jurisdiction to include the exercise of prerogative powers. The language of *ultra vires* is therefore no longer appropriate.

THE BASIS OF INTERVENTION

In the CCSU case, Lord Diplock categorised the basis of intervention as follows:

> Illegality
> Irrationality
> Procedural Impropriety

The effect of the implementation of the Human Rights Act 1998 is to extend even further the grounds for intervention. An example of this is the increasing importance of the doctrine of proportionality which was heralded by Lord Diplock as a potential ground for review.

Illegality

> "By illegality as a ground for judicial review I mean that the decision maker must understand correctly the law that regulates his decision making power and must give effect to it." (*per* Lord Diplock in CCSU, above).

Thus where power is exercised by someone who does not meet the qualifications laid down in the grant of power, the Act may be considered illegal.

In *Allingham v The Minister of Agriculture and Fisheries* (HC, 1948) the Minister had a statutory power to give directions regarding the cultivation of land for agricultural purposes. He had an express power to delegate this function to a committee which, in turn, attempted to further sub-delegate its functions to an executive officer who issued a directive to a farmer that only sugar should be grown in a particular field. The farmer failed to comply with the direction and, when fined, challenged its validity alleging that the executive officer had no power to issue it. The court quashed the conviction finding that only the Minister or the Committee had the power to issue such orders under the statute. In *R. v DPP Ex p. Association of First Division Civil Servants* (DC, 1988) the delegation of certain functions under the Prosecution of Offences Act to non-lawyers was held to be unlawful.

(N.B. The courts will sometimes imply a power to sub-delegate into a statutory provision.) In *Vine v The National Dock Labour Board* (HL, 1957) Lord Somervell of Harrow said that in deciding whether there is such a power, two factors have to be considered:

(a) the nature of the power;

(b) the character of the person.

If the power is of a routine nature the courts will be more willing to imply a power to sub-delegate than if there is a strong element of discretion involved. They have also shown themselves reluctant to allow any sub-delegation of judicial or legislative powers. If the body exercising the power has been established especially for that purpose, the courts are likely to conclude that Parliament intended the body to act personally. Where the power is exercised by a minister, for practical reasons, the courts are more willing to hold that he has an implied power to sub-delegate. (*Carltona v Commissioner of Works* (CA, 1943).) It should be noted, however, that often when a minister acts through his civil servants, there is no delegation. The civil servant is simply acting as the alter ego of the minister. (*R. v Secretary of State for the Home Office Ex p. Oladehinde* (HL, 1990).)

Illegality might also consist of using powers in a manner totally different from that envisaged, as in *Att-Gen v Fulham Corporation* (above). Essentially the task of the court is to determine the nature of the powers granted. In *Commissioners of Customs and Excise v Cure & Deeley* (HC, 1961), Sachs J. said that in carrying out its task, the court was bound to examine "the nature, the objects and scheme of the parent act, and in the light of that examination, to consider what is the area over which power is given." In doing this, there are a number of presumptions of statutory interpretation which can assist the court such as the presumption that a body has no power to act retrospectively and the presumption that a body has no power to restrict a person's access to the courts. (*Chester v Bateson* (HC, 1920) and *R. v. Lord Chancellor Ex p. Witham* (DC, 1997).) Cases such as *Bromley LBC v GLC* (HL, 1982) demonstrate that determining the scope of a body's power is far from being a mechanical task but involves the court in making value judgments.

Another example of improper use of powers occurred in *R. v Secretary of State for Foreign Affairs Ex p. The World Development Movement Ltd* (HL, 1995) where the payment of overseas aid to fund the construction of the Pergau Dam in Malaysia was held to be illegal as it was made for a purpose not envisaged by the relevant statute.

There may often be a requirement that before a body exercises its power a particular state of affairs must exist as a preliminary requirement. If power is exercised without this, the action may be illegal. In *White and Collins v Minister of Health* (CA, 1939) the Local Authority had certain powers of compulsory purchase in relation to land which did not form part of private parkland. This meant that a condition for the exercise of the power was that the land was of the appropriate type. The court held that an attempt by the Local Authority to acquire private parkland was *ultra vires.*

Irrationality

Irrationality is the second ground on which Lord Diplock would exercise the powers of review.

> "It applies to a decision which is so outrageous in its defiance of logic or of accepted moral standards that no sensible person who had applied his mind to the question to be decided could have arrived at it."

This was often referred to in earlier cases as situations where there had been an "abuse of power". (See *Anisminic v Foreign Compensation Commission* (HL, 1969).) The court's concern is about the manner in which the decision has been taken. This category includes such grounds of challenge as unreasonableness, irrelevant considerations and improper motive. It is clear that these are not discrete categories. Irrationality may be approached from a number of perspectives.

Unreasonableness

The courts may review decisions on grounds of "manifest unreasonableness", that is where the decision is so unreasonable that no reasonable person would agree with it. (*Associated Provincial Picture Houses Ltd v Wednesbury Corp.* (CA, 1948).) A widely used example is that of a local authority which decides that in no circumstances would it employ a teacher with red hair. This unreasonableness is recognised in cases such as *Wheeler v Leicester City Council* (HL, 1985) and *R. v Ministry of Defence Ex p. Smith* (CA, 1986) where Sir Thomas Bingham M.R. approved the following:

> "The court may not interfere with the exercise of an administrative discretion on substantive grounds save where the court is satisfied that the decision is unreasonable in the sense that it is beyond the range of responses open to a reasonable decision maker."

Henry L.J. in *R v Lord Chancellor Ex p. Maxwell* (CA, 1996) described a very high standard of unreasonableness saying that decisions that are so unreasonable " jump off the page at you."

Irrelevant considerations

If a body acting under statutory authority takes an irrelevant consideration into account or ignores a relevant consideration then the resultant decision will be open to challenge (*Associated Provincial Picture Houses Ltd v Wednesbury Corp.* (CA, 1948)).

In *Padfield v Minister of Agriculture and Fisheries* (HL, 1968) the Minister had the power to refer complaints about the operation of the Milk Marketing Board scheme to a committee. He refused to refer a complaint of substance to the committee. It subsequently emerged that one reason for his decision was that he had taken into account the fact that publicity about the complaint would be politically damaging for the Government at that time. This, the court said, was an irrelevant consideration which rendered his decision unlawful. Lord Upjohn said that unlawful behaviour might be constituted by:

(a) an outright refusal to consider the relevant matter;
(b) a misdirection on a point of law;
(c) taking into account some wholly irrelevant or extraneous consideration;
(d) wholly omitting to take into account a relevant consideration.

In *R. v Somerset CC Ex p. Fewings* (CA, 1995) a local authority decision to ban stag hunting on its land was quashed. Under its statutory power it was required to take an objective judgment about the proper management of its land. Clearly the ban was imposed because hunting was seen as being morally repulsive. Such ethical considerations were held to be irrelevant in terms of the Local Authority's powers to manage the land.

Essentially the court is concerned whether the decision-making body has addressed itself to all relevant factors. It is not concerned with the question whether proper weight has been given to those factors. (*Pickwell v Camden LBC* (HC, 1983)). But where the decision is reached on the basis of two quite separate considerations, one which is relevant and one which the authority is not entitled to take into account, the court must decide which was the dominant consideration. If this is an irrelevant consideration then the authority's action will be reviewable (*R. v ILEA Ex p. Westminster Council* (HC, 1986)).

Improper purpose

The courts have held that if a public body exercises its statutory power for an improper purpose they can intervene. In *Padfield's* case Lord Reid pointed out that Parliament had given the Minister a discretion as to whether complaints were referred to the committee. It was not, however, an unlimited discretion. He argued that it could be implied that it had been given with the intention that it should be used to promote the policy and objects of the enabling Act. See also *R. v Secretary of State for Foreign Affairs Ex p. World Development Movement Ltd* above, where this aspect of irrationality was also a basis of challenge.

One difficulty is how the courts ascertain the policy of any Act of Parliament. Rarely is this expressed in the statute. In *Padfield*, Lord Reid said that the courts must carry out this task by construing the Act as a whole. Sometimes it is impossible to determine the purpose and no intervention is possible on this ground as, for example, in *British Oxygen Co. Ltd v Minister of Technology* (HL, 1971). On the other hand, in *Congrieve v The Home Office* (CA, 1976) the Minister had a statutory power under the Wireless Telegraphy Act 1949 to revoke television licences. He used this apparently unrestricted power to revoke licences purchased early to avoid an increase. The court held that the Minister had acted *ultra vires* in that he had used his power for an improper purpose. Lord Denning said that it could be implied that the Minister had been given this power only to enable him to revoke licences obtained illegally.

The decision in *Pepper v Hart* (HL, 1993) now makes it possible for the courts to look at Hansard in attempting to ascertain the purpose for which power was given.

Failure to give reasons

One effect of a failure to give reasons for a decision is that it may suggest that there is no good reason and that the resultant decision is irrational. Unreasonableness will not always be inferred from the absence of reasons (*Lonrho plc v Secretary of State* (HL, 1989)) but in *Padfield* (above) Lord Pearce clearly felt that it gave rise to the possibility. Failure to give reasons may also constitute procedural impropriety. (See below.)

Procedural impropriety

Breach of express procedural requirement

The court may review a decision where there has been a failure to comply with express procedural requirements contained in an Act of Parliament or secondary legislation. Examples of such requirements are:

(a) consultation (*R. v Social Services Secretary Ex p. Association of Metropolitan Authorities* (HC, 1986));

(b) the holding of an inquiry to hear objections to a planning application (*Jackson Stansfield v Butterworth* (CA, 1948)).

The effect of non-compliance with a procedural requirement varies, depending on its importance. Traditionally the courts have categorised requirements as either mandatory or directory. Only where the breach is considered to be of a mandatory procedural requirement will non-compliance affect the validity of the exercise of power as in *Agricultural Training Board v Aylesbury Mushrooms* (HC, 1972). Breach of a directory requirement will not affect validity (*R. v Sheer Metalcraft Ltd* (HC, 1948)).

The process of determining whether a particular procedural requirement is mandatory or directory is one of statutory interpretation. What does Parliament intend to be the result of the breach? Of course, Parliament rarely provides express guidance and the court must assess the importance of the requirement and its relationship to the general purpose of the statutory framework in which it is set. (Lord Penzance in *Howard v Bodington* (HL, 1877).)

However, in *London & Clydeside Estates Ltd v Aberdeen DC* (HL, 1980), Lord Hailsham criticised a too rigid distinction between mandatory and directory procedural requirements. Not only was it often difficult to ascertain Parliament's intention but the significance of a breach might vary with the circumstances of each case. He said that the court was faced with a spectrum of possibilities. At one end there were serious procedural defects which would render any decision a nullity. Other defects were so trivial as to have no effect. But in the middle, cases would arise where the courts had to exercise their discretion, cases where differences of degree merged almost imperceptibly into differences of kind.

Thus in *Secretary of State for Trade and Industry v Langridge* (CA, 1991), Balcombe L.J. considered the following in determining the effect of non-compliance with a procedural requirement:

(i) the importance of the relevant procedural requirement;
(ii) the relation of that requirement to the general object intended to be secured by the Act; and
(iii) the relevant circumstances of the case.

Lord Woolf in *R. v The Home Secretary, Ex p. Jeyeanthan* (1999), suggested that the court must also consider whether substantial compliance would fulfil the requisite procedural requirements and whether non compliance was capable of being waived.

Breach of implied procedural requirements

The courts have implied such requirements as a requirement to consult (CCSU case), a requirement to give reasons (see below) and the duty to follow a fair procedure.

Implied requirements of fairness

Historically the concept of fairness was tied up with the rules of natural justice which were traditionally applied to judicial decisions. There were two aspects to the rules, both referred to by Latin tags:

1. The *Nemo Judex* rule—no man should be a judge in his own cause.
2. The *Audi Alteram Partem* rule—the right to a fair hearing.

For much of the twentieth century the courts restricted natural justice to judicial decisions taken by court like bodies. The case of *Ridge v Baldwin* (HL, 1964) opened up the application of the rules of natural justice to a much wider range of circumstances. The Chief Constable of Brighton was dismissed from office by the Brighton Watch Committee without an adequate hearing. Did natural justice apply? The decision clearly affected the Chief Constable's legal rights for no better reason than that it would affect pension rights. It could, however, be argued that the Watch Committee was acting in an executive or administrative capacity rather than judicially. Lord Reid, however, greatly extended the scope of natural justice by requiring the Watch

Committee to give the Chief Constable a fair hearing, arguing that justice demanded it.

The courts subsequently extended the scope of natural justice beyond judicial decisions. In the CCSU case, for example, Lord Scarman indicated there was an implied duty of fairness attached to all administrative acts. In *Doody v The Home Secretary* (HL, 1993), Lord Mustill said that where an Act of Parliament confers an administrative power there is a presumption that it will be exercised in a manner which is fair.

The requirement of Art.6 of the ECHR that "in the determination of his civil rights and obligations or of any criminal charge against him, everyone is entitled to a fair and public hearing within a reasonable time by an independent and impartial tribunal", imposes a further requirement of fair decision making.

What standard of fairness will be required will vary depending on the type of decision, who takes it and the circumstances. As Lord Mustill pointed out in Doody, "what fairness demands is dependent on the context of the decision."

The Nemo Judex rule—the rule against bias

If the judge has a pecuniary interest in the outcome of a case then he is absolutely barred from hearing it. There is no need to show actual bias. The mere existence of the interest is sufficient to disqualify the judge—*Dimes v Grand Junction Canal* (HL, 1852). A direct pecuniary or proprietary interest, however small, is conclusively presumed to create a real danger of bias (per Sedley J. in *R. v Secretary of State for the Environment Ex p. Kirkstall Valley Campaign Ltd* (DC, 1996). The interest must not be too remote. *R. v Rand* (HC, 1866).

This automatic disqualification was extended in *R. v Bow Street Magistrates Ex p. Pinochet* (HL, 1999), beyond the situation where the judge had a pecuniary or direct proprietary interest in the case. The judge had an involvement with Amnesty and it had presented evidence in the case.

Other interests that may disqualify a judge from acting, include family relationships (*Metropolitan Properties v Lannon* (CA, 1969)); and business connection (*R. v Sussex Justices Ex p. McCarthy* (HC, 1924)). It may be that these now constitute automatic disqualifications. (*Locabail (UK) Ltd v Bayfield Properties Ltd* (CA.2000).)

A second situation is where the circumstances surrounding the case suggest in some way that the judge was biased. Perhaps it appeared that he had already made up his mind before taking the decision. In *Ex p. Hook* (CA, 1976), for example, it was clearly wrong that the person making the allegations against the market-trader should participate in the decision as to whether he should lose his licence. He would be acting both as a prosecutor and as a judge. Perhaps he had expressed an opinion on the matter. As the court said in *Locabail*:

> "It would be dangerous and futile to attempt to define or list the factors which may give rise to a real danger of bias. Everything will depend on the facts".

In this second situation while it is not necessary to establish actual bias, it is necessary to show that the decision has given the appearance of bias. In *Sussex Justices* the court said that "it is of fundamental importance that justice should not only be done but should manifestly and undoubtedly be seen to be done."

How is the test of bias formulated? In *R. v Gough* (HL, 1994) the House of Lords formulated the following test: *was there a real danger of bias by the decision-maker.*

This was further explained in *R. v Inner West London Coroner Ex p. Dallaglio* (CA, 1994) where the court said that in reaching its conclusion the court personified the reasonable man." In *Re Medicaments and Related Classes of Goods (No.2)* (CA, 2001), the court reviewed the *Gough* test to ensure it was in line with convention requirements and the approach taken by the European Court of Human Rights. It felt that, in general, the two approaches coincided, subject to a modest adjustment to the Gough test to emphasise that the court was applying an objective test in the circumstances and not making a judgment on the likelihood of a particular tribunal being, in fact, biased. Lord Steyn in *Magill v Porter & Weeks* (HL, 2001) summed up the position by saying that "the question is whether the fair minded and informed observer, having considered the facts, would conclude that there was a real danger of bias."

The Human Rights Act

The effect of the Human Rights Act is that where Art.6(1) applies, there is a right to an independent and impartial tribunal. The ECHR in *Findlay v UK* (1997) said that in considering the independence of such a tribunal, they would look at how the judges were appointed, their term of office and whether they were subject to any pressures which might influence them.

The UK system of Courts Martial was accordingly found not to be convention compliant.

In the Scottish case of *Starrs v The Procurator Fiscal Linlithgow* (1999), it was held that the system of appointing Temporary Sheriffs breached the Convention. They had no security of tenure and their appointments were subject to annual renewal by the Lord Advocate, a member of the Government.

In *McGonnell v UK* (ECHR 2000), the role of the Deputy Bailiff of Guernsey, which combined executive and judicial functions, was such as to cast doubt on his independence when dealing with a planning matter. The question whether the Secretary of State for the Environment, Transport and the Regions had the requisite independence when dealing with certain planning matters was considered by the House of Lords in the Alconbury Case (*R. v Environment Secretary Ex p. Holdings and Barnes* 2001). It was argued that, as the Secretary of State laid down planning policy and issued guidance and framework directions which local authorities and the Planning Inspectorate must follow, he could not act as an independent judge when dealing with disputes. However the House of Lords advised that there was no violation of Art.6 as any decision by the Secretary of State was appropriately subject to judicial review.

In *R. v the Home Secretary Ex p. Anderson and Taylor* (HL, 2002), the House of Lords declared that s.29 of the Crime (Sentences) Act 1997 which allowed the Home Secretary to fix the tariff element of a mandatory life sentence, was incompatible with Art.6.

The audi alteram partem rule—the right to a fair hearing

It is impossible to lay down precisely the contents of this rule as this may vary depending on the circumstances and the type of function being exercised. As Lord Bridge said in *Lloyd v McMahon* (HL, 1987):

> "what the requirements of fairness demand . . . depends on the character of the decision making body, the kind of decision it has to make and the statutory or other framework in which it operates."

Thus in *McInnes v Onslow Fane* (HC, 1978), for example, a contrast was drawn between cases involving forfeiture of a licence, renewal cases and initial applications. In the first two instances there was a legitimate expectation of being granted a hearing but not in the case of an initial application where minimal standards of fairness applied. But where an initial application would only be refused, *e.g.* because of allegations against the applicant, justice might require he be given a hearing to answer any such allegations.

The minimum requirement is that the person must have an adequate opportunity of presenting his case. (*Local Government Board v Arlidge* (HL, 1915).) This does not mean that a person is always entitled to an oral hearing (*R. v Criminal Injuries Compensation Board Ex p. Dickson* (CA, 1996)). In *SP v Secretary of State for the Home Department* (HC, 2004), fairness required that a prisoner should be allowed to make representations before he was segregated within a young offenders' institution unless, in the circumstances it would be contrary to good order and discipline to allow him that right.

The courts are concerned to see that there is equality of treatment between the parties. So, for example, the rule was broken when the court heard one side in the absence of the other. (*Errington v Minister of Health* (CA, 1935).) In *R. v National Lottery Commission Ex p. Camelot Group Plc* (HC, 2000), the court quashed the decision of the Lottery Commission to exclude Camelot from further negotiations on lottery rights. It said that the procedure had been conspicuously unfair as a result of "a marked lack of even-handedness between the parties".

A person must also have adequate notice of any charges to be brought against him or any matters that have to be taken into account. (*Kanda v Government of Malaya* (PC, 1962)). The court said:

> "If the right to be heard is a real right which is worth anything, it must carry with it a right in the accused man to know the case which is made against him. He must know what evidence has been given and what statements have been made affecting him, and then he must be given a fair opportunity to correct or contradict them."

In *R. v Secretary of State for the Home Department Ex p. Georghiades* (DC, 1992), the court said that justice and fairness required that a prisoner should be told why his parole licence had been revoked to enable him to present his case to the Parole Board.

A person must have a reasonable time to prepare his case. In *R. v Thames Magistrates Ex p. Polemis* (HC, 1974) the court held that if a person had been given insufficient time, an adjournment must be granted.

The tribunal need not always observe the strict procedures of a court of justice. In *R. v Commissioner for Racial Equality Ex p.*

Cottrell (HC, 1980) it was said that as the function being exercised was more administrative than judicial the attendance and cross-examination of witnesses, from whom statements had been taken, at a formal hearing was unnecessary. Contrast this with *R. v Board of Visitors of Hull Prison Ex p. St Germain No.2* (HC, 1979) where it was said that persons charged with serious disciplinary offences had a right to call any evidence which was likely to assist in establishing vital facts in issue, that the chairman had a discretion to refuse to call witnesses to prevent the accused calling so many witnesses as to make the system unworkable but that fairness demanded that there be a right to cross-examine witnesses.

The courts do not appear to consider that legal assistance is an absolute requirement of the rule although there is a readiness to imply it if procedural rules are silent. Legal assistance may not necessarily involve legal representation as an oral hearing is not always necessary.

A long standing principle in administrative law has been that tribunals should develop appropriate procedures and these are not necessarily modeled on court-like procedures. Legal representation may have the effect of formalising the procedure where the aim is to make the decision maker approachable and informal. So should the courts interfere where a tribunal makes a rule preventing legal representation? Lord Denning has gone further than any other judge in demonstrating a willingness to require legal representation even where this is prohibited by the procedural rules governing the body in question (see, *e.g. Pett v Greyhound Racing Association* (CA, 1969)). His views were criticised by the House of Lords, for example in *Pett No. 2* (HL, 1970) and even he held in *Maynard v Osmond* (CA, 1977) that legal representation was not an absolute requirement where a police officer who was facing disciplinary charges was denied legal representation under the Police Disciplinary Regulations. The officer was, however, entitled to assistance from another officer.

R. v Board of Visitors of Wormwood Scrubs Prison Ex p. Anderson (HC, 1983) held that the Board of Visitors should have exercised its discretion to allow legal representation in view of the seriousness of the charges and the potential penalty, the need for fairness between the parties involved and the ability of the prisoners to represent themselves. Other relevant factors might be the complexity of the case and whether any points of law were likely to arise. See also *R. v Board of Visitors of HM Prison, The Maze Ex p. Hone* (HL, 1988).

Article 6(3)(a) of the ECHR provides that everyone charged with a criminal offence has a right to defend himself through legal assistance.

The duty to give reasons

One particular requirement of fairness might be a duty to give reasons in support of a decision. In *R. v Higher Education Funding Council Ex p. Institute of Dental Surgery* (CA, 1994), it was held that there was no general duty to give reasons but it depended on the individual circumstances. Factors identified as relevant as to whether such a duty would be implied were:

(a) where the decision involved an interest which was highly regarded in law such as personal liberty (see *R. v Ministry of Defence Ex p. Murray* (DC, 1997);
(b) where the nature of the process required reasons to be given (see *R. v Secretary of State Ex p. Doody* (HL, 1994);
(c) from the circumstances of the individual case (see *R. v Civil Service Appeal Board Ex p. Cunningham* (CA, 1992).

It is now clear that where the decision constitutes a determination which affects an individual's civil rights and obligations, Art.6 (10) of the ECHR requires the decision maker to give a reasoned judgment.

Beyond Wednesbury unreasonableness

Art.13 of the ECHR requires subscribing states to provide an effective remedy to those claiming their rights have been infringed. In cases such as *Smith and Grady v UK* (2000 ECHR) the European Court of Human Rights has found that judicial review on grounds of "Wednesbury unreasonableness" did not provide an effective remedy. This is despite the fact that in cases involving interference with personal rights, the English courts have indicated that they would give the issue "anxious or heightened scrutiny" and adopt a lower threshold of unreasonableness than that normally applied. (See *R. v Ministry of Defence Ex p. Smith* (CA, 1996) and *R. v Lord Saville of Newdigate Ex p., A* (CA, 1999).)

In *R. (Mahmood) v The Home Secretary* (CA, 2001), the Court of Appeal considered the proper standard for intervention on grounds of unreasonableness. Lord Justice Laws emphasized that the courts should not consider the merits of the decision for then they would be acting as a court of appeal. Whether they adopted the lower threshold as expounded in *Smith* or the more stringent approach in *Wednesbury* depended on the subject matter of the dispute. However, to satisfy the ECHR, it would seem that the court would have to come close to looking at the merits of the decision.

In *R. v The Home Secretary Ex p. Daly* (HL, 2001), Lord Steyn felt that the test of unreasonableness needed to be further developed and suggested that the court, in deciding whether a decision was unreasonable, might consider whether it was proportionate.

Proportionality

In the CCSU case, Lord Diplock had suggested that the principle of "proportionality" which has long been part of the jurisprudence of EC law and the ECHR might develop into a ground of judicial review in English law.

Proportionality is concerned with balance and whether the means justify the ends. It has been described by the Committee of Ministers of the Council of Europe in 1980 as follows:

> "An appropriate balance must be maintained between the adverse effects which an administrative authority's decision may have on the rights, liberties or interests of the person concerned and the purpose which the authority is seeking to pursue."

Proportionality as a ground of challenge was recognised by Lord Slynn of Hadley in the *Alconbury* case (*R. (Alconbury Developments Ltd) v Secretary of State for Transport, Environment and the regions* (HL 2001).

> "I consider that . . . the time has come to recognise that this principle [proportionality] . . . is part of English administrative law, . . . even when dealing with acts under domestic law."

The doctrine of proportionality may require the reviewing court to assess the balance which the decision-maker has struck, not merely whether it is within the range of rational or reasonable decisions. As such it may go further than the traditional grounds of review as it may require attention to be directed to the relative weight to be attached to the various factors involved. Yet Lord Steyn in *Daly* felt that proportionality added little to the concept of unreasonableness. The courts continue to struggle with the need to satisfy the vigorous review demanded by Art.13 yet maintain the traditional refusal to consider the merits of the decision.

7. REMEDIES

JUDICIAL REVIEW THE AVAILABLE REMEDIES

These fall into two groups, the prerogative orders (quashing, prohibiting and mandatory orders) and the non-prerogative remedies (declaration and injunction).

The prerogative orders

These orders (formerly writs) were originally brought by the King against his officers to compel them to exercise their functions properly or to prevent them abusing their powers. They are remedies of public law. As such, historically, they were not available to control the activities of private bodies or domestic tribunals.

Quashing order

A quashing order (formerly certiorari), is used to quash the decisions of inferior courts, tribunals, local authorities and other public bodies, government ministers, etc:

  (a) on grounds of illegality, irrationality and procedural impropriety;
  (b) where there is error of law.

In *R. v Northumberland Compensation Appeal Tribunal Ex p. Shaw* (CA, 1952) the tribunal, assessing the amount of compensation owed to Shaw, misinterpreted the statutory provisions and made an error of law which was apparent on the face of the record of the decision. That decision was quashed. The error need no longer be on the face of the record. (See *R. v Hull University Visitor Ex p. Page* (HL, 1993).)

While formerly confined to judicial decisions affecting a person's legal rights, it has been granted to control licensing decisions—*R. v Barnsley MBC Ex p. Hook* (CA, 1976); in *R. v Paddington Valuation Officer Ex p. Peachey Property Corp. Ltd* (CA, 1966), to challenge an exercise of power by a valuation officer in compiling the valuation list; and in *R. v London Borough of Hillingdon Ex p. Royco Homes Ltd* (HC, 1974), to quash the granting of planning permission. It would therefore be inaccurate today to say that certiorari would not lie to control the exercise of an administrative function.

Prohibiting order

A Prohibiting Order (formerly prohibition), is used to restrain a tribunal, minister or other public body from proceeding in excess of jurisdiction. For example in *R. v Liverpool Corp. Ex p. Liverpool Taxi fleet Operators Association* (CA, 1972) it was alleged that a local authority had failed to exercise its discretion properly and was about to act illegally in the allocation of taxi cab licences. A prohibiting order was granted to prevent the authority acting on this invalid decision.

In general its scope is similar to that of a quashing order.

Mandatory order

A Mandatory Order (formerly mandamus), is an order which commands a person or body to perform a public duty. Typically it is used to compel the exercise of a duty imposed by statute on a public body. For example, in *R. v Manchester Corp* (HC, 1911) the order compelled the local authority to make bye-laws that it was under a statutory duty to make.

A mandatory order cannot be directed to the Crown as such as the Crown is not commandable (*R. v Secretary of State for War* (CA, 1891).) Nor can it be issued against any servant of the Crown acting in his capacity as servant. But where, by statute, an officer of the Crown has an independent public duty towards a member of the public, the order may lie to compel performance of that duty. Thus a distinction is drawn between a duty imposed on the Crown and a duty imposed on a named Crown servant.

Non-prerogative orders

There are two remedies, the declaration and the injunction, which are not primarily remedies of public law but are widely used in this field.

Declaration

A declaration is a convenient and flexible remedy available in both public and private law matters which can be used to obtain a statement of the legal relationship between parties in a wide range of circumstances. It can be used, for example,

    (a) to challenge the legality of administrative decisions. (*Ridge v Baldwin* (HL, 1964));

    (b) to challenge the validity of delegated legislation. (*Daymond v South West Water Authority* (HL, 1976));

    (c) to establish the existence or the scope of a public duty. (*Central Electricity Board v Jennaway* (HC, 1959));

    (d) Declaratory judgments can be made against the Crown.

It is not necessary for the claimant to show that he has some subsisting cause of action or a right to some other relief. (*Gouriet v Union of Post Office Workers* (HL, 1978).) *R. v Secretary of State for Employment Ex p. Equal Opportunities Commission* (HL, 1994) made it clear that the court still has the power to make a declaratory judgment in judicial review proceedings whether or not it could also make a prerogative order.

Restrictions on the use of the declaration

    (a) The claimant must have a right or interest which is justiciable.

    (b) There must be a real dispute between the parties. The court will not attempt to resolve an academic matter (*R. v Secretary of State for Employment Ex p. Equal Opportunities Commission* (HL, 1994)).

    (c) As a declaration will not quash a decision, it cannot be used to challenge a decision on the ground that there has been an error of law on the face of the record of the tribunal's decision as this is an error within jurisdiction. A declaration that such a decision is irregular would still leave the decision intact. *Punton v Minister of Pensions and National Insurance No.2* (HL, 1963).

    (d) Interim declarations cannot be made.

Injunction

This is an order by the courts, either prohibiting the party to whom it is addressed from doing a particular act, or requiring the party in question to perform a particular act. Accordingly injunctions can be either prohibitory or mandatory. It can be used:

(a) To prohibit a body from acting *ultra vires*. In *Bradbury v Enfield LBC* (CA, 1967) an injunction was granted to prevent a local authority from reorganising local schools without following the correct procedure;

(b) In *Att-Gen, ex relator McWhirter v IBA* (CA, 1973), an application was made for an injunction to restrain breaches of statutory duty;

(c) Mandatory injunctions are much less common in public law as mandatory orders are normally a more appropriate remedy, but they have been granted, for example, to require public bodies to enforce planning regulations and fire precautions.

Restrictions on the use of the injunction

Under the Crown Proceedings Act 1947, s.21(1), a final injunction will not be awarded against the Crown or one of its officers, although this has little practical importance as the Crown will abide by the terms of a declaration. (The major difficulty has been the inability to obtain interim relief.)

In the express context of Community law, the House of Lords in *Factortame Ltd (No.2)* (HL, 1991), disregarded the rule precluding such interim relief in national law, in order to give protection to the rights claimed under Community law. In *M v Home Office* (HL, 1994), the possibility of interim relief against ministers and government departments acting in the name of the Crown was recognised.

CLAIMS FOR REVIEW

Up till 1977, the procedures for applying for prerogative and non-prerogative remedies were entirely separate. Significant changes were made in 1977 with the introduction of the application for judicial review.

A number of changes were made to Order 53 of the Rules of the Supreme Court under which applications for prerogative orders were made. This was initially by regulation and then by s.31 of the Supreme Court Act 1981. Following the Woolf reforms and the Bowman Committee Report, a new procedure for making claims was introduced in October 2000 and can be found in Pt 54 of the Civil Procedure Rules. Judicial review procedure (JRP) is also subject to the overriding objectives contained in Pt 1 of the CPR.

The procedure for applying for judicial review

The judicial review pre-action protocol first requires the exchange or pre-action letters. Claimants make an umbrella claim for judicial review. Within this claim, it is possible to ask for any of the above remedies either singly, in any combination and in the alternative. See, for example, *R. v The Inland Revenue Commissioners Ex p. Rossminster* (HL, 1980). Damages can also be awarded where appropriate, *e.g.* for Human Rights breaches.

Claimants do not have to choose which route to pursue, and may leave it to the court to provide the most appropriate remedy.

There is a two stage procedure for making the application:

(a) Application for Permission.

The claimant must ask for permission to apply for judicial review. The court will generally in the first instance consider a question of permission without a hearing. A hearing is likely to be requested if the claim involves a point of law likely to require some argument, if interim relief is sought or if the judge wishes to give guidance on a matter of public interest.

The notice of claim will be accompanied by an affidavit containing all the basic factual material on the application. The claim form must be served on the defendant.

The purpose of this filter stage is to weed out hopeless cases at the earliest possible time, thus saving pressure on the courts and needless expense for the claimant. For example, it allows malicious and futile claims to be weeded out and prevents public bodies being paralysed for months because of pending court action.

In order to obtain leave, the claimant must satisfy the court that he has, on the face of it, an arguable case and has the necessary standing to make the claim. Where permission is refused there is provision for renewal of the claim and a right of appeal. The exact procedure varies depending on whether it is a civil or criminal matter and whether there has been an oral hearing.

The requirement to seek permission is a significant filter but is being operated with considerable variation. Some judges examine the claim at length at this stage. Others content themselves with a quick look. Research has indicated that no common criteria are being applied. Despite this the new procedural rules say nothing about the criteria for the grant of permission.

(b) The Hearing.

The Hearing takes place in the Administrative Court of the Queen's Bench Division and will normally be before two judges in a criminal case. In civil matters the case will normally be heard by a single judge sitting in open court. In very important cases, three judges may sit. It may even be decided without a hearing if the parties agree.

The main source of evidence will be sworn affidavits. The court has the power to take oral evidence and to permit cross-examination although this is unusual.

Discretionary nature of remedies

The court has a discretion as to whether to grant relief. Factors which might persuade the court to refuse the application are:

(i) the availability of an alternative remedy. (*R. v Birmingham City Council Ex p. Ferrero Ltd* (CA, 1993).) But if the alternative remedy is inappropriate in the circumstances the JRP may be used. (*R. v Chief Constable of Merseyside Ex p. Calveley* (CA, 1986));

(ii) where review would serve no useful purpose as the decision, properly taken, would be the same. (*R. v Monopolies and Mergers Commission Ex p. Argyll Group Plc* (CA, 1986));

(iii) where the court does not like the motives of the applicant (*R. v Customs and Excise Commissioners Ex p. Cooke & Stevenson* (HL, 1970));

Non-Justiciability

Sometimes the courts will consider it inappropriate to exercise their power of judicial review on the basis that the nature of the dispute is such that it does not lend itself to resolution by a judicial type of process. This arises if the matter involves a balancing exercise which judges, by their experience, feel ill-qualified to perform. Examples given include disputes involving the making of treaties, the defence of the Realm and the grant of honours. (See Lord Diplock in the CCSU case.) However in *R. v Minister of Defence Ex p. Smith* (CA, 1996), it was said that "only the rarest cases would today be ruled strictly beyond the court's purview, that is only those cases involving national security where the courts lacked the experience or material to form a judgement on the issues."

It has been suggested that the influence of the Human Rights Act 1998 might be such as to prevent the court from refusing to interfere on this ground but in *Secretary of State for the Home Department Ex p. Isiko* (CA, 2001), it was emphasised that the concept of non-justiciability remained relevant and that there were still areas of judgements considered by democratically elected bodies which necessarily commanded deference from the courts. So, for example, in *R. (On the application of CND) v The Prime Minister*, (1993), the courts refused to review the Prime Minister's decision to invade Iraq.

Time limits for making an application

Under r.54(5), a claim must be made promptly and in any event not later than three months after the grounds for the application first arose. This must be read together with s.31(6) of the Supreme Court Act 1981 which says that the court may refuse an application for review on ground of undue delay if it considers that the granting of the relief would be likely to cause substantial hardship to, or substantially prejudice the rights of, any person, or would be detrimental to good administration. It would therefore appear that:

(a) There is no three month entitlement for a quashing order and an application made within the three month period could be refused for delay if, under s.31(6) the granting of the relief was, for example, detrimental to good administration (*R. v Dairy Produce Quota Tribunal Ex p. Caswell* (CA, 1989)), or if it would substantially prejudice the rights of another. (*R. v Secretary of State for Health and Another Ex p. Furneaux and others* (CA, 1994).)

(b) The previous procedural rules under Order 53 did allow an extension to the three month period for good reason. For example, in *R. v Stratford-on-Avon DC Ex p. Jackson* (CA, 1985) the delay in making the application arose mainly because of difficulty in obtaining legal aid. The court was satisfied that the circumstances constituted a good reason for extending the period. In *Re S* (CA, 1997) where S had been detained under the Mental Health Act 1983, following her refusal to consent to a Caesarean section, the question was considered to be of such public importance that leave was granted despite the delay in applying. Rule 54(5) does not repeat this power to extend the period but there is a general power under r.3(1)(2)(a). Even if an applicant convinced the court that there was good reason for extending the three month period, the application may still fail by virtue of s.31(6).

The short period available within which a claim may be brought may render the time limits vulnerable to challenge under the Human Rights Act. (*R. (Burkett) v Hammersmith & Fulham LBC* (2002).)

The requirements of standing

Only a claimant who has the requisite standing may apply for judicial review. Prior to the 1977 reforms, the test of standing was clearly different for the various remedies. The Law Commission recommended that there should be one test of standing for all the remedies, that a claimant should have such interest as the court considers sufficient in the matter to which the application relates. Section 31(3) of the Supreme Court Act 1981 provides that the court will not grant leave for JRP unless the claimant has sufficient interest in the matter to which the application relates.

What constitutes sufficient interest?

The House of Lords considered this in *R. v IRC Ex p. The National Federation of Self Employed and Small Businesses Ltd* (1982). The applicants wished to challenge an alleged amnesty granted to casual workers in the newspaper industry who had been avoiding paying tax for many years. Quite clearly this decision did not affect the applicants' legal rights. But did they have a sufficient interest?

The House of Lords (Lord Diplock dissenting) advised that they had not. The following points arose:

(a) The majority felt that the applicants' standing could not be considered in the abstract but only in conjunction with the merits of the case. Only in a few extreme cases could applications be weeded out for lack of standing at the filter stage.

(b) Thus a connection was drawn between the sufficiency of the interest and the seriousness of the illegality complained of. The more serious the illegality, the more liberal the rules of standing.

(c) Their Lordships were divided as to the extent to which they were constrained by the pre-1977 authorities in determining the question of standing. Lord Diplock alone felt that they had an unfettered discretion. The majority felt that they had to pay some attention to the earlier law but were divided as to the precise weight to be accorded to it.

(d) A similar divergence of views was seen on whether there is a uniform test of standing. Those judges who felt most bound by the earlier authorities were led to the conclusion that the test varied from remedy to remedy. In contrast Lords Diplock and Roskill saw the main purpose of the reforms as being to sweep away procedural differences between the various remedies.

The House of Lords accepted that it was not necessary that the applicants' legal rights were affected. According to Lord Scarman the test was whether "there is a genuine grievance reasonably asserted." He stressed the relationship between the sufficiency of the applicants' interest in relation to the subject matter of the application. Lord Fraser emphasised that a mere busybody would lack sufficient interest but gave little guidance as to how one distinguishes the busybody from the person with a reasonable concern.

Decisions since the *IRC* case have confirmed that a liberal approach to standing should be taken. Only claims by busybodies should be excluded. For example the interest of a business competitor was recognised in *R. v Department of Transport Ex p. Presvac Engineering Ltd* (CA, 1991). So too persons may have the requisite interest as a result of "legitimate expectation that they will be heard," perhaps arising out of assurances given or knowledge of general practice (*O'Reilly v Mackman* (HL, 1983)).

In many cases the courts have allowed pressure groups to apply for judicial review. (*R. v Hammersmith & Fulham LBC Ex p. People Before Profit Ltd* (DC, 1981). *R. v HM Inspectorate of Pollution Ex p. Greenpeace* (DC, 1994) held that Greenpeace had standing to challenge the variation of existing authorisations for the Sellafield nuclear processing site by reason of its membership in the area.

The courts have also recognised a claimant's interest on the basis that the claimant had " a sincere concern" for constitutional issues, (*e.g.* where William Rees-Mogg was permitted to challenge the ratification of the Maastricht Treaty.

In *R. v Secretary of State for Foreign Affairs Ex p. World Development Movement* (HL, 1995), the question of standing was raised at first instance. Rose L.J. accepted that the applicants had standing on the basis of the importance of the issues raised, the likely absence of any other responsible challenger and the role of the applicant in giving advice on the grant of aid.

Thus in determining whether the applicant has standing the courts consider:

(a) the merits of the application;
(b) the nature of the applicant's interest;
(c) all the circumstances of the case.

The current procedural rules do not say anything new about standing but they give the court power to permit any person to file evidence or make representations at a hearing. (54.17 CPR). This follows the approach which allowed Amnesty to make representations during the Pinochet hearing.

Who is amenable to judicial review?

The supervisory jurisdiction of the High Court is over bodies exercising public law functions. In *(R. (Heather) v Leonard Cheshire Foundation* (CA, 2002) the court found that the Foundation was not a public body and disallowed the claim for judicial review. Traditionally public bodies have been established by statute or through an exercise of the royal prerogative. In *R. v City Panel on Take-overs and Mergers Ex p. Datafin Plc* (CA, 1987), judicial review was sought to challenge the decision of an unincorporated association which exercised no statutory or prerogative powers. Indeed Lord Donaldson M.R. described it as "a body performing its functions without any means of judicial support." It was successful.

The justification for this is often that the body is carrying out a function, which, if it did not perform it, would be carried out by the Government. A further justification might be that the function is closely enmeshed with a public function. (*Poplar Housing and Regeneration Community Association Ltd v Donoghue* (CA, 2002).)

Conversely, not every public body will be subject to review with regard to every action it takes—only if it is a public matter. (See *R. v BBC Ex p. Lavelle* (CA, 1983) which stressed that where public bodies carried out purely managerial functions, the exercise of such functions were not amenable to judicial review.

In *R. v Chief Rabbi Ex p. Wachmann* (DC, 1992), the court held that the exercise of a disciplinary function by the Chief Rabbi was not susceptible to judicial review.

An exclusive procedure?

Clearly the procedure described above must be used to obtain a prerogative order. But in the case of a declaration or an injunction, does the applicant have the choice in a public law matter to use another form of procedure?

In *O'Reilly v Mackman* (HL, 1982) an attempt to obtain a declaration by way of action that a Board of Visitors had acted contrary to the rules of natural justice in hearing disciplinary charges against a prisoner, was struck out as an abuse of process. Section 31(2) of the Supreme Court Act 1981 provides that a declaration may be obtained by means of an application for review where the High Court considers it would be just and convenient having regard to:

(a) the nature of the matters in respect of which relief may be granted by way of the prerogative orders;
(b) the nature of the persons and bodies against whom relief may be granted;
(c) all the circumstances of the case.

The court was satisfied that, in the circumstances, relief could have been granted by way of a prerogative order. It was clearly a public law matter and would be more appropriate to use the judicial review procedure as it provided safeguards against frivolous applications, for example through the need to apply for leave. Their Lordships felt that although it was not the exclusive procedure for raising such a matter it would generally be the most appropriate. As had been pointed out in the Court of Appeal, there was a clear need to develop a comprehensive method of handling such cases and the Divisional Court had particular expertise in the area.

It was suggested that there were three circumstances where the judicial review procedure might be inappropriate:

(a) where the matter was collateral to another application. (Applied in *Cocks v Thanet DC* (HL, 1982));
(b) where public law issues are raised as a defence to criminal charges. (See *Wandsworth LBC v Winder* (CA, 1985));
(c) otherwise on a case-to-case basis. It may be inappropriate to use the judicial review procedure in a complex Chancery matter for example.

Subsequent cases led to concern that the existence of a public law element, however slight, was forcing litigants to use the judicial review procedure and deprive them of the right to bring an action for private law relief. *Roy v Kensington & Chelsea & Westminster Family Practitioner Committee* (HL, 1992) represented a retreat from this exclusivity principle. The House of Lords identified two approaches:

(i) a broad approach under which Order 53 would only be insisted on if private rights were not in issue;
(ii) a narrow approach which required applicants to proceed by the judicial review procedure in all proceedings in which public law matters are challenged subject to those exceptions already noted.

It followed the broad approach and found the fact that there was an incidental public law matter did not prevent the litigant from seeking to establish his right by action. This approach has been confirmed by the House of Lords in *R. v Secretary of State for Employment Ex p. EOC* (HL, 1994) and *Mercury Communications Ltd v Director General of Telecommunications* (HL, 1996) and in *Clark v University of Lincolnshire and Humberside* (CA, 2000) where the court was not willing to strike out a claim simply because it might have been more appropriate to bring it by way of judicial review. Lord Woolf identified as the crucial factor whether the protections afforded by the judicial review procedure had been flouted in circumstances which were inconsistent with the general principles contained in the CPR Pt 1.

The new CPR Pt 54 does not provide any further guidance. English law still lacks any comprehensive definition of public law. The mere fact that one of the parties involved is a public body is not, of itself, sufficient. In *R. v Panel of Take-overs and Mergers Ex p. Datafin plc* (CA, 1987), the court said that in considering whether it was a public law matter, the court must not only consider the source of a body's powers and duties but also their nature. Do these have a "Public element" or was its sole source of power a "consensual submission to its jurisdiction"?

NON-JUDICIAL REMEDIES

The individual who has a complaint against the administration may chose to use a non-judicial route. He may ask his MP to raise the matter with the Minister, *e.g.* through a written or oral question in Parliament (see Ch.3). This allows discussion of the merits of the decision in a way not available in judicial review. He may approach one of the Commissioners for Administration and request that the matter be investigated. This allows a consideration of whether there has been maladministration, a term which covers a range of situations much wider than those which give rise to judicial review.

In addition to the Parliamentary Commissioner for Administration, there are now a separate Scottish Parliamentary Commissioner and Welsh Administration Ombudsman, Health Service Commissioners for England, Wales and Scotland, Local Government Commissioners for England, Wales and Scotland, a Legal Services Commissioner, and a European Union and Community Ombudsman. Indeed the idea has also been adopted in the private sector, for example in Banking.

THE PARLIAMENTARY COMMISSIONER

Following considerable pressure to establish a mechanism to investigate complaints by members of the public who felt that they had suffered injustice at the hands of Central Government, the Parliamentary Commissioner Act 1967 was passed providing for the appointment of a Commissioner to investigate complaints of maladministration by those government bodies and public authorities listed in the Act. A separate Local Government Commission was established under the Local Government Act 1974 to investigate maladministration by local government departments. Thus the PC cannot investigate local government or the police.

The office

He is a Crown appointment. He holds office during good behaviour, but may be removed by the Crown following addresses from both Houses of Parliament. His status is similar to that of a judge in terms of independence. He has the power to appoint his own staff, subject to Treasury control over numbers and conditions of service.

Terms of reference

To investigate all complaints of maladministration by those departments listed in Schedule 1 of the 1987 Parliamentary and Health Service Commissioners Act as amended by the Parliamentary Commissioner Act 1994. The Schedule lists not only government departments such as the Home Office and the Inland Revenue, but also non-departmental bodies such as the Arts Council. Since 1994 he has also dealt with problems arising out of the obtaining of information in accordance with the Codes of Access to Government Information. Following the Freedom of Information Act 2000, complaints which are wholly or mainly about access to information will be dealt with by a new Information Commissioner who is likely to become operational in 2005.

He cannot look into the activities of the police, the nationalised industries, or the Cabinet Office.

Maladministration

Maladministration is not defined in the Act. It appears that the intention was to allow the PC guided by the Select Committee on the Parliamentary Commissioner, to work out a practical definition.

Maladministration has been defined as "any kind of administrative shortcoming, poor administration or the wrong application of rules."

Richard Crossman, speaking during the Second Reading debate on the passage of the Bill through the Commons said, in what has become known as the "Crossman Catalogue", that maladministration might include "bias, neglect, inattention, delay, incompetence, ineptitude, perversity, turpitude, arbitrariness and so on." In *R. v Local Commissioner for Administration North East England Ex p. Bradford MCC* (CA, 1979), a case involving the jurisdiction of the Local Commission which has similar terms of reference, Lord Denning accepted the Crossman catalogue as an adequate description of the scope of the term.

At first the PC interpreted his terms of reference rather narrowly refusing to question the quality of discretionary decisions even where these appeared biased or perverse. Gradually, he began to consider certain discretionary decisions where there is evidence of maladministration in the way the discretion was exercised.

The following have been found to constitute maladministration:

(a) failure to provide necessary information and advice;
(b) failure to provide an adequate explanation;
(c) provision of inadequate or misleading information and advice;
(d) basing decision on false or inadequate information, ignoring relevant evidence;
(e) avoidable delay;
(f) faulty procedures or failure to follow departmental rules and procedures;
(g) rudeness and inconsiderate behaviour by officials;
(h) bias or prejudice;
(i) failure to monitor faulty procedures, *e.g.* DTI monitoring of Barlow Clowes.

Exclusions

1. Section 12(3) of the Act expressly excludes consideration of the merits of the decision. The rationale for this is that policy matters are the exclusive concern of Parliament. Note, however, the difficulty of distinguishing questions of merit and policy from the way in which the decision has been reached. (*Ex p. Bradford MCC*, above).
2. The PC is excluded from considering those matters listed in the Third Schedule of the Act. These include:
   (a) Actions affecting relations with other governments or international organisations.
   (b) Actions taken under the Extradition Act 1989 or the Fugitive Offenders Act 1967.
   (c) Administration of territories overseas.
   (d) Security and passport matters, criminal investigations.
   (e) Commencement or conduct of legal proceedings.
   (f) The exercise of the prerogative of mercy.
   (g) Actions taken in relation to contractual or other commercial transactions excluding certain matters relating to compulsory purchase.

(h) Personnel matters relating to those bodies covered by the Act.

(i) The grant of honours, awards and privileges within the gift of the Crown.

Restrictions (g) and (h) have been widely criticised.

3. The PC will not normally investigate a matter for which the complainant has a legal remedy before the courts unless there is doubt about its availability or to pursue the remedy would be slow or expensive.

4. The PC can only investigate the exercise of administrative functions. He cannot investigate judicial or legislative (s.12(3)).

5. He has refused to investigate matters which he considers to be purely political, *e.g.* the allocation of time between political parties for party political broadcasts.

Investigation of complaints

Complaints to the PC are confidential and his investigations are private. The service is free. Complaints must be channeled through MPs not necessarily the complainant's own. As there is concern that this might deter complainants it has been suggested that it should be possible to approach the PC directly. The Select Committee rejected this arguing that the PC would be overwhelmed with complaints and that it would undermine the role of the MP in looking after the interests of his constituents. The response to this might be that if there was a dramatic increase in the number of complaints resources should be made available to deal with them. Not all MPs deal with complaints effectively. Indeed they lack the resources to do so. It is surely more important to safeguard the interests of constituents than to pander to the sensibilities of MPs. In any event it would not prevent constituents enlisting the help of their MP if they so wished.

In fact, since 1978, the PC has, if approached directly, offered to send the complaint to an MP asking for it to be returned. This appears to work quite satisfactorily.

In 2003–4, the PC's workload was down slightly on the previous two years at 2319 cases. Forty-one per cent of these complaints related to the Department of Work and Pensions and its related agencies such as the Child Support Agency and Jobcentre Plus. The Inland revenue, The Treasury and the Home Office also featured regularly. Common themes were handling errors, delays, misdirection or poor handling of complaints.

The Annual report shows that 72 complaints were outside his jurisdiction, 738 concluded on the basis of the papers, 498 resolved without a positive outcome, 421 resolved positively on the complaint being raised with the department in question, 64 under investigation and only 84 subject to a full statutory investigation leading to a report before Parliament. Work was still in progress on a further 442.

If the PC decides to conduct an investigation, he must, under s.7(1), give the department concerned the opportunity of commenting on any allegations made. The investigation is conducted in private by a member of his staff. There are wide powers of investigation, a right to question ministers and civil servants, a right to look at all necessary documents. The right to go into the department in question and examine files is of considerable value. He is denied access only to Cabinet Papers, a restriction which the PC has said is no real practical hindrance. The duty to assist him overrides any obligation to maintain secrecy under the Official Secrets Acts. Under s.11, the Minister can give the PC notice that the publication of certain information would be prejudicial to the interests of the State. The Minister cannot, however, veto the investigation.

The case of *R. v Parliamentary Commissioner for Administration Ex p. Dyer* (DC, 1994) illustrates the reluctance of the courts to review the way the PC carries out his functions. Only in extreme cases of abuse of power might they intervene. They were, in general, unwilling to interfere with the exercise of his discretion.

The result of the investigation

The Commissioner sends a report to the MP, the department investigated and any other person concerned. If indeed maladministration has been established, the report will suggest what action might be taken to remedy it. Sometimes this may be a financial payment, sometimes that a decision be reversed, sometimes an apology. (See, for example, the *ex gratia* payments made by the Government following the Commissioner's Report on the Barlow Clowes case and payments made by the Inland Revenue following late payments as a result of problems with a new computer system at the Contributions Agency.)

The PC does not have any direct sanction. He cannot enforce his recommendations. Under s.10(3) he may, however, lay a special report before Parliament as he did following an investigation into the Transport Department's handling of the Channel Tunnel Rail link. He is then dependent on the weight of opinion pressurising the department in question to comply with his recommendations.

As well as suggesting a remedy for the individual complainant, the Commissioner is equally concerned to suggest administrative changes which would prevent the occurrence of maladministration in the future.

The PC must make an Annual report to Parliament and his work is monitored by the House of Commons Public Administration Select Committee.

Assessment

The PC remains a little-known figure whose reports attract minimal publicity. Although the number of complaints has risen steadily in recent years, this is still a much smaller number than anticipated and fewer per head of population than received by ombudsmen abroad. The many limitations on his jurisdiction noted above and his lack of sanction both serve to limit his effectiveness. He cannot be approached directly and he has no power to initiate investigations.

Nevertheless, he has often managed to obtain compensation for complainants or persuaded departments to review their decisions and he has had considerable success in persuading departments to change their administrative procedures although the caution of many of his recommendations may be determined by what he knows he can achieve. A continual tension is whether he should concentrate his resources on obtaining redress in individual cases or should he devote his time to improving general standards of administration? It has been argued that the lack of sanction is a positive feature in persuading departments to co-operate and not close ranks against the investigators. Out of the glare of publicity they may be more willing to admit mistakes.

8. SAMPLE QUESTIONS AND MODEL ANSWERS

It should be assumed that questions are answered in 45 minutes under examination conditions.

Question 1

"Parliament has under the English constitution, the right to make or unmake any law whatever; and no person or body is recognised by the law of England as having a right to override or set aside the legislation of Parliament."

Answer

1. Explanation of Dicey's view:

Parliament can make laws on any subject affecting anyone, anywhere.

The courts must give effect to the latest intention of Parliament—there is no hierarchy of laws.

The courts have no power to challenge the validity of an Act of Parliament. (*British Rail Board v Pickin* (HL, 1974).)

2. Consideration of whether Parliament still has freedom of action to make or unmake any law

i. Note the effect of membership of the EU.

Note the view of the ECJ that, by joining the EU, Member States have limited their sovereign rights (*Costa v ENEL* 1964). Under the treaty obligations, within those areas regulated by Community law Member States have obligations to reconcile domestic law with Community law and their courts must give effect to Community law. In the eyes of the ECJ Community law has a higher status than domestic law. (*e.g. Simmenthal*).

Section 2(4) of the 1972 Act appears to accept the hierarchical approach. (*Factortame.*) Explanation that the logical effect of this is to limit the Westminster Parliament's freedom of action in that if it legislated contrary to Community law there would be an obligation on the courts to disregard such conflicting legislation even where this represented the latest intention of the UK Parliament.

Describe the attitude of the UK courts showing how this has developed through cases such as *Garland* and *Macarthys v Smith* to *Factortame* where Parliament was forced to repeal the Merchant Shipping Act and provisions of the Crown Proceedings Act were disapplied.

ii. Consideration of the Human Rights Act

The ECHR has not been fully incorporated into our law in the same way as Community law. It should be noted that Parliament still retains the right to legislate contrary to the Convention. The Human Rights Act simply imposes an obligation to declare whether the legislation is compliant or not. Nevertheless it imposes a significant moral and political pressure on governments to comply. In addition s.3(1) of the HRA requires the court to adopt an approach to interpretation which might require the judge to ignore the intention of Parliament in order to construe the provision in a way which accords with the convention.

3. Conclusion

Dicey's concept of supremacy must clearly be modified in the light of the above. *Factortame* has shown the extent the courts are prepared to go in ensuring the supremacy of Community law. However it must be noted that

- As yet the courts have not been required to declare an act invalid as being contrary to Community law
- They have no power to declare legislation invalid in contexts other than Community law
- Under the HRA the courts have no power to declare legislation invalid but can only issue a declaration of incompatibility. It is then up to the Government to act.

Argue that the 1972 Act is not entrenched (see Denning in *Macarthys*) and that while the doctrine of implied repeal has been modified, there still appears to be the power to repeal it expressly thus preserving some aspects of Dicey's concept of supremacy.

Question 2

The Westminster Parliament is no longer at the heart of the political and government processes in the United Kingdom and plays an ever-decreasing role in calling the Government to account.
  Discuss.

Answer

Consideration of the factors which have restricted the central role of the Westminster Parliament:

(i)   Influence of the EU.
(ii) Devolution.
(iii) Changes in House of Lords which have limited its credibility.
(iv) Governments with large majorities and weak opposition have taken the spotlight off Parliament.
(v)   Increased tendency to announce policy outside the House.
(vi) Government control over Parliament through whip system, patronage, control of timetable, etc.—possibly strengthened as a result of the modernisation changes.

Although it should be noted that in formal legal terms Parliament still provides the Government and must approve legislation, grant of supply and taxation.

Consider whether Parliament's role in calling the Government to account has diminished. Consider:

(i)   Practical significance of ministerial responsibility—minister's response to criticism—naming and blaming civil servants; sheltering behind chief executives of next step agencies; the lack of relationship between fault and resignation.
(ii) Effectiveness of questioning ministers—the use of written and oral questions—the ability to avoid answering; government control over information; the use of PM's question time; question time used for other purposes.
(iii) Traditional opportunities for scrutiny and their hmitations; the Government majority, the Whip system and control of the timetable; lack of publicity, *e.g.* adjournment debates.
(iv) Effectiveness of select committees—more effective scrutiny because of specialist knowledge, ability to call witnesses, select topic, production of information, etc. But N.B. reliance on Parliament to compel attendance; particular problem in obtaining answers from civil servants who are accountable to their Minister; no systematic scrutiny of expenditure.

Conclusion

It may be useful to note in conclusion that effective scrutiny depends on knowing the questions to ask and having access to relevant information reference could be made to Parliamentary

Resolutions on openness and accountability and Questions and Procedures for Ministers re duty of disclosure to the House.

Question 3

One evening the police receive reports that two youths have stolen cigarettes and some money from an old age pensioner who had just bought them at a local corner shop. He described them as quite small, wearing dark shell suits and one had a red baseball cap. Half an hour later PC Smith sees three boys smoking outside the shop. They are known to him as "trouble-makers". They are all wearing shell suits but none are wearing caps.

He orders them to turn out their pockets which they grudgingly do. Nothing untoward is found. While the search is taking place, one of the youths ostentatiously drops a crisp packet on the ground at the officer's feet. He refuses to pick it up and tells the officer what to do with the crisp packet!

At this point the officer bundles the youth into a police car and tells him he is under arrest. Consider the legality of the police conduct.

Answer

1. Consider whether PC Smith has the power to order the youths to turn out their pockets?

- (i) There may be a power to stop and search for stolen goods under s.1(2)(a) of PACE 1984.
- (ii) The officer must have reasonable grounds for suspecting that he will find stolen goods (s.1(3)).
- (iii) Code of Practice on Stop and Search emphasises that whether the police have reasonable grounds for the stop and search depends on the circumstances of the case but they must have an objective basis, *i.e.* one which would appear justifiable and reasonable to a third party. Thus PC Smith can rely on the description of the alleged offenders, their presence in the vicinity, their demeanour. He can take into account his knowledge of them in conjunction with the other information noted above. He cannot rely on personal factors alone *e.g.* their bad reputation plus appearing a stereotyped offender.

You should reach a conclusion on this noting that the fact nothing was found is irrelevant. It was whether the officer had reasonable grounds at the time he embarked on the search.

2. Assuming there was a power to stop and search has the search been carried out properly in terms of the Act?

(i) The search should be carried out courteously.

(ii) If PC Smith is not in uniform, he must supply documentary evidence, s.2(2)(b).

(iii) He should have provided the information required in s.2(3).

(iv) Having carried out the search, PC Smith should have completed a record of the search in accordance with s.3 and recorded the information required in s.3(6). There appears to be no reason to exclude this requirement under s.3(1) or to delay making it under s.3(2).

(v) The power would entitle the police officer to ask the boys to turn out their pockets. He has not infringed s.2(9)(a).

It appears that while the extent of the search was lawful, the formalities which are designed to protect suspects have not been complied with.

3. The validity of the "arrest"—the grounds?

(i) Note that the police have a summary power of arrest under ss.24 and 25 of PACE and at common law to prevent the continuance of a breach of the peace. No arrestable offence appears to have been committed. (You may choose to define this.) Most likely power under s.25.

(ii) Examine the s.25 power noting that the constable must suspect that an offence must have been committed, etc., and that service of a summons would be impracticable or inappropriate because one of the general arrest conditions applies. Examine the general arrest conditions in s.25(3) and consider whether any of these apply to this situation and conclude whether there are legal grounds for the arrest.

4. Have the formalities been complied with for a valid arrest?

(i) The youth has been informed that he is under arrest s.28(1).

(ii) He has not been informed of the grounds of the arrest s.28(3). This is required even if the facts are obvious s.28(4). There appears to be no justification for delaying the giving of this information in accordance with s.28(5).

(iii) Consider whether the officer has used unjustifiable force.

Conclusion

Question 4

Sam earns a living by selling ice-cream from a van in the city of Oldtown. It is a requirement that he has a valid trading licence from Oldtown Council. In May 2001, Oldtown City Council opened a Leisure Centre which, among other things, sells ice cream and soft drinks. Sam sells ice-cream from his van outside the Leisure Centre every Saturday and Sunday afternoon. On Saturday August 9, Sam is told to move his ice-cream van away by an official of the Leisure Centre. He refuses in no uncertain language and the following day sells ice-cream there as usual. On Tuesday August 12, he receives a letter from Oldtown City Council telling Sam that his licence to sell ice-cream is revoked as from Friday August 15. No reason is given.

Sam appeals against this decision and is told he can appear in person before a special meeting of the Licence Appeals Committee on Monday August 18. He is refused legal representation at the hearing and is prevented by the chairman from cross-examining witnesses. The decision to remove his licence is confirmed by the Appeals Committee whose Chairman is manager of the Oldtown Leisure Centre. Again no reasons are given for this decision.

Advise Sam.

Answer

Consider the possibility of applying for judicial review of the decision to remove Sam's licence on ground of procedural impropriety.

1. Is there an implied requirement that Sam should have had a fair hearing?

Note that this is a licensing decision which has been analysed as relating to a privilege. It does not affect his legal rights. Nevertheless in cases such as *McInnes v Onslow Fane* and *Ex p. Hook* the courts have implied a requirement that there be a fair hearing. The nature of this will vary depending on whether it is an initial application where minimal standards will apply or renewal or revocation cases where the requirements will be much more stringent. Note the various justifications for this including "legitimate expectation of a hearing; the seriousness of the consequences as Sam is being deprived of his livelihood and the fact that, as allegations have been made against him, justice demands that he has a right to answer these allegations".

2. The decisions should have been taken by an unbiased judge.

Although the connection appears too remote to amount to a direct pecuniary interest, the Chairman may have a non-pecuniary interest through his business connection with the Leisure Centre and possibly through acting as complainant and judge.

Consider and apply the appropriate test of bias, as *per R. v Gough.*

3. Consider whether Sam has been given a fair hearing

(a) Has he been adequately informed of the complaint against him?

(b) Does fairness demand legal representation in the circumstances and a right to cross-examine witnesses? (Note the requirement of equality of treatment between the parties.)

(c) Lack of reasons may suggest that the decision was irrational. The courts will readily imply a right to a reasoned decision (*Ex p. Doody*) as the possibility of appealing depends on this information.

Question 5

The office of Parliamentary Commissioner for Administration was established to provide a remedy for the citizen who has suffered as a result of maladministration by Central Government. What advantages does this have over pre-existing judicial and parliamentary remedies? In what ways could the Parliamentary Commissioner's effectiveness be increased?

Answer

Prior to the establishment of the office of Parliamentary Commissioner in 1967, the citizen complaining of maladministration could either:

(a) complain to an MP;
(b) pursue a legal remedy in the courts.

The Critchel Down Affair illustrated the limitations of these methods. The PC appears to have certain advantages.

Advantage over MPs action

1. The PC is not hampered by any political allegiance but is independent.
2. The PC has greater ability to determine how the decision was reached.

Note. His powers of investigation (s.7). MPs may question ministers but have limited power and opportunity to force the minister to disclose more than he wishes. The Sachsenhausen Concentration Camp case illustrates the way in which the PC's wider powers of investigation prove more effective, in particular his right of access to departmental files and the fact that he is not restricted by the Official Secrets Acts.

Advantage over judicial remedies

1. The PC investigates complaints of maladministration. The meaning of this term should be discussed and it should be noted that it is wider than the range of administrative defects open to investigation by the courts who can intervene only:
   (a) in the circumstances outlined in the CCSU case (illegality, irrationality, procedural impropriety and proportionality);
   (b) where there is an error of law;
   (c) where there is a statutory right of appeal;
   (d) where there has been a breach of a convention right.

   Although the involvement of the courts in administrative decision making has increased in recent years as a result of
   (a) the extension of the application of the rules of natural justice to a wider range of situations and the development of the implied requirement of a right to a fair hearing;
   (b) the development of the concept of abuse of power and the increased control of the courts over discretionary decision making; the courts cannot be said to

provide a comprehensive review of the activities of the administration;

(c) The Human Rights Act 1998.

2. The court is concerned with giving a remedy to the individual applicant. The PC is also concerned with improving the general standard of administration in the department in question.

3. The court will reach its decision on the basis of the evidence presented to it by the parties. The Crown may even attempt to rely on public interest immunity to prevent information being made available. Contrast this with the wide investigative powers of the PC.

It should, of course, be noted that where there is a legal remedy the PC will not normally investigate.

The PC's effectiveness could be increased in the following ways:

1. By increasing his jurisdiction:
   (a) By expanding the definition of "maladministration" to enable him to investigate "any unreasonable, unjust or oppressive action."
   (b) By removing the restrictions in Sch.3, *e.g.* by allowing the PC to investigate contractual and commercial matters involving government departments.
   (c) By allowing the PC to investigate more freely disputes where there might also be a legal remedy.

2. By making him more accessible:
   (a) Discuss the possibility of removing the MP filter.
   (b) Consider how public awareness of his role might be increased, noting the low level of complaints presently investigated.

3. By giving the PC an effective sanction. Describe his present powers to ensure his recommendations are implemented. These could be contrasted with those of the Northern Ireland Commissioner.

4. By allowing him to initiate investigations.

INDEX

(All references are to page number)